Interoperability for Enterprise Information Systems

Alea Fairchild

Computer Technology Research Corp.
6 North Atlantic Wharf, Charleston, South Carolina 29401 U.S.A.
Telephone: (803) 853-6460 • Fax: (803) 853-7210 • E-mail: reports@ctrcorp.com

Interoperability for Enterprise Information Systems

Copyright © Computer Technology Research Corp.

First Edition - 1996

ISBN 1-56607-975-6

Published by Computer Technology Research Corp., Charleston, South Carolina U.S.A.

Library of Congress Cataloging-in-Publication Data

Fairchild, Alea
    Interoperability for enterprise information systems / Alea Fairchild. -- 1st ed.
        p. cm.
      ISBN 1-56607-975-6
       1. Management information systems. 2. Internetworking (Telecommunication) I. Title.
      T58.6.F25 1996
  650' .0285--dc20   96-30866
                                              CIP

INTEROPERABILITY FOR ENTERPRISE INFORMATION SYSTEMS

TABLE OF CONTENTS

LIST OF FIGURES

LIST OF TABLES

Introduction

Certain cultures have several words for a particular concept that reflects both its physical attributes and the importance of its place in peoples' lives. The language spoken by Eskimos, for example, has numerous words that refer to the concept of "snow," and each term signifies a different type of snow or associated quality. In technical terms, however, there is only one word for "interoperability," although it has come to represent a variety of connectivity attributes between different computers.

Information technology (IT) professionals have yet to create a descriptive language that captures the complexity of enterprise computing. Like those languages with only one word for rain, their speech relies on one all-encompassing term to describe the gentle quiet of a well-tuned system to the storm of user irritation when interconnection creates more problems than answers. What does the word "interoperability" really mean, and is there a composition and concept that can bring a useful order to its many different meanings?

The term interoperability was first coined in the late 1960s by multinational military groups such as the North Atlantic Treaty Organization (NATO). The term was invented to encapsulate the idea — which was quite unique at the time — of designing the weapons of other countries' forces to use similar ammunition. The idea: Cooperating forces should be able to share key resources, rather than being forced to maintain separate stocks of what should be common supplies.

The same process carries over to the corporate sector, where information replaces weapons as the valuable resource available to any of the cooperating groups. Information is expensive to collect, verify, and maintain, yet many companies have been continually unsuccessful in building systems and networks that demonstrate any awareness of the merits of sharing those costs.

Yet, spreading long-term costs often incurs initial costs. However, one hopes the net present value of the benefits will be greater than the initial costs of data translators, portable user-interface libraries, and tools over the entire life cycle of a corporate computing architecture.

Interoperability drives down the technology costs. When applications are designed to operate on any number of different computers, hardware becomes a commodity. As new network capacity is available, solutions from many vendors can be considered because there are few conversion costs to consider when moving open applications from one vendor's system to that of another. As systems and networks become "scalable," users can increase the capabilities of their IT enterprise at will, transparent to the applications.

However, interoperability should not be the goal in itself. The purpose of initial costs and investments is to avoid future, often hidden costs of other approaches, and to add to the business advantage of the enterprise itself.

The purpose of this report is to describe the business issues within the realm of interoperability and to suggest solutions to challenges through the examination of each of the technology areas and the related industry standards involved. Interoperability affects all areas of technology, including hardware portability, software development, and especially communications. The role of the Internet in interoperability will be critical as more companies go online. The result will be a changing organization structure with different priorities and different objectives.

While the benefits of interoperability are obvious to the IT manager, the business benefits must be quantified and justified for the business units they support. These benefits may be difficult to achieve in the short-term, but are necessary for the long-term survival of the dynamic IT environment. The challenge of interoperability in today's organization combines the business need for information, the unique differentiation of competitive advantages that IT provide, and the changing nature of how companies do business.

The chapters contained in this report are:

1. Executive Summary
2. The Management of Interoperability

3. Hardware Platforms and Portability

4. Software Development and Maintenance

5. Connectivity and Communication

6. Internet and Intranet Interoperability Issues

7. Information Management

8. Resource Needs

9. Future Trends

10. Conclusion

The Executive Summary describes the benefits provided by interoperability, discusses some of the standards that organizations such as the Open Software Foundation (OSF) have imposed so as to have assisted the interoperability cause, and summarizes the management and organizational issues, as well as the technical challenges, that make interoperability an ambitious goal for many enterprises.

Chapter 2 explains how one manages the increasing level of complexity interoperability requires, focusing on the technological and managerial issues affecting the success of interoperability in the enterprise. Managing interoperability means the combining of business and technological objectives to create added value to the organization. This organization encompasses the entire enterprise, including international operations, mobile workers, extended partners and suppliers.

Chapter 3 provides a discussion on the basic compatibility level many organizations try to achieve. It examines the available choices for managing hardware: In-house expertise, outsourcing to one or many IT consultants or turning to the hardware vendors for support. This chapter also discusses operating system (OS) compatibility and how the mind set of industry has turned away from the operating systems or platform toward the application and its development.

Chapter 4 extends the discussion of application development and focuses on the value of software development to the enterprise and various approaches and standards in software development. Object-oriented programming (OOP), database management, and the standardization of development components such as common object request broker architecture (CORBA), object linking and embedding (OLE), and distributed computing environment (DCE) are areas of vendor discussion. In this light, additional necessities such as middleware, common application programming interfaces (API), and the maintenance of software are also examined.

Chapter 5 provides the framework for arguably the most discussed part of interoperability – the network. Network communications, inside and outside the enterprise, is an area where standards are constantly evolving as technology progresses. This chapter examines the choices of integrated services digital network (ISDN), asynchronous transfer mode (ATM), Frame Relay (FR), Fast Ethernet, and situations where their uses are most appropriate. It also provides an examination of the application areas of groupware, messaging, and video conferencing to see how industry standards are assisting the efforts of these collaborative approaches. Finally, the chapter discusses the integration efforts between connectivity and communication throughout the enterprise domain via local area networks (LANs), wide area networks (WANs), and global telecommunications.

Today's great hope for interoperability is the Internet and intranets. Chapter 6, which discusses this phenomena, focuses on managing usage and content from both an internal and external aspect. Planning a successful Internet strategy for the enterprise involves clearly outlining business goals and defining areas of concern such as bandwidth availability and security. This chapter also discusses hardware and software choices, implementation, and Web site and intranet maintenance.

Chapter 7 examines the crucial role of information in the enterprise. The information systems (IS) management has become strategic to the business enterprise as technology advances increase its competitive positioning. A number of issues are essential to business strategies and the investment in information technology. This chapter focuses on the use of data management strategies such as data warehousing and data drills, and the sharing and reuse of information within the organization via print management, storage management, and commonalties across the company.

Chapter 8 discusses the most efficient use of information technology (IT) and IT staff resources within a company. It focuses on outsourcing and outsourcing management, asset management for controlling IT equipment costs, the costs and benefits of migration and customization, and the management of IT personnel in a time when resources are stretched and budgets are slim.

Chapter 9, which looks at future trends, examines three particular areas of interest for the future of interoperable organizations: The Internet, the desktop, and the use of IT as a competitive advantage for business. As IT becomes more mainstream in business, its usage and the backbones of infrastructure that support it demonstrate that technology is just another business tool that needs proper implementation to be used effectively.

Interoperability is more than an integration of technologies, it is the installation of methodology and procedures to enhance the viability of technologies' usage in the enterprise. Technology will ultimately become as commonplace in the work environment as the pencil and pen – once the organizational and structural aspects of technology are put into place. A solid foundation of correctly implemented technology provides today's dynamic enterprise an additional tool for surpassing the competition.

Chapter 1

Executive Summary

According to the Institute of Electrical and Electronic Engineers' (IEEE's) portable operating system interface for UNIX (POSIX) committee, the key to open systems is interoperability, defined as the ability to run on a wide range of platforms, interoperating with the applications of those systems via a consistent interface. If one extends that definition across the technologies of the enterprise, interoperability can be defined as the possibility to use systems, applications, and networks within an extended organization's IT environment. Because technology and standards are constantly evolving, one can look at interoperability as something to be achieved, but not necessarily something achievable. Interoperability can also be thought of as the ability of different systems to be linked together and then operate as a single entity.

With the "mad dash" onto the Internet, the confusion regarding messaging standards and concern over ways to access legacy data are interoperability issues. Standards, methodologies, and approaches all factor into the technology usage in the enterprise. The planning and implementation of technology in business is the key to interoperability in terms of successful IT utilization and enhancement of business advantage.

The rise of the interoperability concept in the enterprise environment is due to the multiple benefits of interconnecting computing equipment from a variety of manufacturers. Interoperable computing allows end-users to utilize almost any platform to do productive work because they know their output can be combined with data and work performed on other platforms. Interoperability is an enabler allowing a much greater degree of collaboration and effective resource usage. It helps IT management make economical purchases based on the capability to use sources from many different suppliers. Interoperable equipment and services increase productivity and cut costs previously associated with proprietary systems and networks.

Working Definitions

There are many working definitions of interoperability at the standards organization level such as "a program-friendly exchange of information." For organizations such as government bodies, for example, it is referred to more in the way of a coordination function rather than an interconnection of sorts.

An excellent working definition, taken from a white paper from Unisys Corporation, is:

"Interoperability is the ability to bridge from the hardware and software components of one vendor to the hardware and software components of another vendor. It also refers to the ability to bridge between software components on the same system. Interoperability defines the mission and promise of IT. By creating a seamless information infrastructure that delivers information 'on demand,' interoperability helps an enterprise concentrate on its business processes, decision making, and customer service. It sweeps away the complex procedures that slow down end-users and prevent them from accessing the information they need. Users are free to focus on their jobs, not on the complexities of computer systems."

Interoperability can be an exchange, a bridge, an interconnection, but more importantly it is a methodology or an approach to computing and networking. Creating this seamless information structure happens by using a concentrated approach and a methodological plan of the structure before, during, and after it evolves.

Segmented by technology platform, interoperability comes in many forms. For example, hardware interoperability refers to the portability and compatibility of data formats – even at the binary level – between different programs or implementations of the same programs on different systems. In communications, interoperability can be obtained by agreeing on standard messaging formats, which are formal specifications that describe the structuring of data to enable transfer and handling of the data by electronic means.

The Internet, by definition, was created to allow interoperability between different computers running different operating systems and applications. This interaction is achieved with HyperText Mark-up Language (HTML) and networking protocols. Although many people try to understand interoperability from a business perspective, it helps to understand the importance of the underpinnings put in place by the standards organizations and vendor bodies.

The Role of Standards

Standards are the key part of the interoperability picture. A wide variety of standards organizations include the Consultative Committee for International Telephony and Telegraphy (CCITT), the International Standards Organization (ISO), the American National Standards Institute (ANSI), and the IEEE. One of the most recent entries is the Worldwide Electronic Messaging Association (WEMA), a collaboration of several regional electronic messaging bodies.

One of the preeminent standards bodies has been the Open Software Foundation (OSF), which has played a critical role in the evolving operating systems space. The OSF was founded in 1988 to respond to user requirements for vendor-neutral open systems solutions. OSF has been driven by member demand, with its membership open to all IT users in business. The OSF is a group of more than 375 users and computer manufacturers, including IBM, Digital Equipment Corp. (DEC), Bull Worldwide Information Systems, Siemens A.G., Phillips Electronics NV, and Hewlett-Packard (HP). It has published several important standards such as OSF/1, DCE, and Distributed Management Environment (DME). The OSF Distributed Computing Environment (DCE) is an integrated, standards-based tool and techniques set that allows distribution of an application's components across a network of heterogeneous computer systems.

General-purpose standards to support interoperability are complex and comprehensive. Such standards usually rely on other standards or families of related standards to provide true interoperability. Attempts to achieve interoperability are typically undertaken by application-oriented groups (for example, in electronic publishing, medical imaging or electronic commerce). However, interoperability standards must be carefully designed to retain the appropriate amount of semantics needed to truly interchange applications data.

According to suppliers such as Microsoft, however, recent history has proven markets to be the fastest and most efficient mechanism for defining interoperability and its implementation. They feel standards-setting organizations can and should agree on interoperable interfaces as they are validated by the marketplace. Others feel standards are best created by industry players on a voluntary basis, but within the structure of international standards bodies. A reasonable assumption: Market forces created by users, and industry knowledge suggested by vendors, both influence standards.

The role of standards within the implementation of interoperability is key because the same basic principals of operation are necessary for two or more entities to share and cooperate. Just as a standard language is necessary for a conversation, a standard framework is necessary for communication and resource-sharing. The need for standards to achieve effective communication and information transfer is clear, and IS users and vendors are committed to the general concept, but not always the specifics.

Management of Interoperability

Managing the need for collaboration and data exchange across the enterprise involves the technological aspects of the interchange and also organizational and structural aspects. Organizations are currently more dynamic in nature, and part of the drive for interoperability is the need to effectively communicate across a decentralized organizational structure, which includes suppliers, outsourcing partners, and mobile workers. To that end, companies must focus on how to establish a strategic solution model for the enterprise environment. This solution should support their operational, organizational, and technological evolution. This model must perform several tasks:

- Leverage existing multivendor systems and accommodate future growth

- Improve the efficiency of business operations, allowing people to share information and corporate resources regardless of location and computing platform

- Support a decentralized organization and centralized data and resources

- Provide secure, reliable, and manageable enterprise communications

- Increase profitability

Profitability and business benefit increases are key measurements for non-IT business management in terms of interoperability assessment. Interoperability entails costs and benefits, however, because designing a system that interoperates with a multitude of other systems may initially be costly. Interoperability is a customer consideration or value in acquiring an advanced information system, but it is not the only requirement. Speed, security, flexibility, innovation, cost-effectiveness, ease-of-use, and other values may be more important to some customers.

Interoperability can be viewed in terms of different sets of business benefits:

- End-users gain from interoperability by enabling them to use any hardware system (PC, terminal, Internet appliance [in the future]) and to accomplish productive work

- IT management benefits by providing opportunities to link information on one system with data mining applications on another and a report-output system on yet another – all without the trial-and-error usually associated in making such a connection

- Senior IT managers can define their own IT purchasing policies regardless of supplier approach and can view technology more strategically than tactically

Interoperability can also be viewed in terms of equipment and service benefits, for example:

- *Hardware:* At the desktop level, a user has a greater choice of desktop "appliances." They can also configure their systems based on personal preference, not necessarily system need, due to network servers.

- *Software:* With common application programming interfaces (APIs), shared, real-time data resources are possible, in addition to accessing information stored on disparate system databases via data mining and warehousing. Interoperability also can mean sharing data without changing data format.

- *Communication:* A company utilizing proprietary mainframes might be able to communicate and exchange data with a company using different client/server (C/S) systems via standard communication protocols.

Interoperability makes productivity more effective by making the IT environment more consistent. Systems that provide a standard end-user interface are known to provide productivity gains because users do not require hours of training or adjustment each time their application is moved to a different platform. Adopting to standard graphical user interfaces (GUIs) will allow users to be presented with consistent interfaces.

The biggest change interoperability represents in the enterprise is the need for a fresh mind-set. In the past, the IT department was centralized and isolated from the actual business it supported. It never needed outside managerial support, it never encountered opposition or had to forge alliances. IT managers must now align business objectives with their own objectives, learn "the business," and cooperate with others to provide a more comprehensive set of services and products for the enterprise. Distributed functions, remote access, and object-based applications are technological challenges based upon business dynamics and needs. The future of interoperability lies in the intertwining of business and technology for an efficient use of resources and a competitive edge in the marketplace.

Chapter 2

The Management of Interoperability

Delivering mission-critical service to business environments and controlling the service within the company is difficult. Add to that challenge the increased use of public networks, diverse desktops, server operating systems, and varying IT and business management philosophies on how to deal with adversity and performance issues. The pressure builds.

How does one manage the increasing level of complexity interoperability requires? Many issues involved are more organizational than technical. With the fast-paced changes in both IT and the organization, it is easy to relax into the familiar, comfortable ways of doing internal business when the dynamic environment demands otherwise. Turning a corporate IT culture around is not an easy task. The success in a legacy, centralized background did not arm IT with many of the skill sets critical to success in today's competitive environment.

Many managers remain skeptical about the claims and perceived territorial considerations of technologists. IT departments are often "fighting the fires" of the technology legacy and it is difficult to find the time – let alone the energy, resources, knowledge or skills – to make the transition to the new technology. As they become more familiar with the potential capabilities of computing, business managers will need to forge tighter working relationships with their IT counterparts.

Two of the key issues for managing interoperability facing today's IT departments are: Managing the scope of the enterprise and continuously moving toward new technologies, new business, and technological objectives.

In managing the enterprise scope, an IT manager must now include international operations and associated logistics, telecommuters, "road warriors" (those workers who are continuously on the road for business), remote operations, and the increasing circle of clients and suppliers who need access to the company server. For meeting objectives, IT managers must try to "hit a moving target," which requires a semi-methodological approach for goal setting and strategies.

Interoperability: Managing the Entire Enterprise

What does the enterprise contain? With the merger-mania of the late 1980s, this may include acquisitions and mergers, partnerships, supplier chains, and customer service databases for external access. Beginning in the late 1980s, companies quickly acquired technology, often without assessing its strategic role in the organization. Therefore, one can find PCs in one department, Macintoshes (Macs) in another, and smart terminals in a third department.

In this heterogeneous, multivendor landscape, IT managers and users alike are calling for interoperability (defined as the assurance products from different vendors will work together). Throwing away previous technology investments and starting from scratch is both financially and productively unacceptable. Rather, companies must leverage their investment in existing technology – including legacy equipment – to build an enterprise computing system. Ensuring products coexist peacefully on a network and operate according to specification will not solve the fundamental problems corporations are addressing. No matter how standardized networking and computing become in the next decade, IT managers will always grapple with the complexities of a multiplatform, multi-operating system world.

The rapid, tactical adoption of desktop technologies driven primarily by users has given way to a more strategic, corporatewide emphasis on networking. General management, IT management, and users are assessing how networks can help them locally and globally to share information, maximize operational efficiency, increase revenue and profits, and maintain a competitive edge to meet strategic business goals. The adoption of C/S computing is not enough. Customers need a new generation of integrated network services. Currently, the network environment consists of heterogeneous, multivendor platforms and applications used primarily on an individual basis. Customers need a new solution model to build a truly interoperable enterprise IS that benefits the business. This solution model requires an enterprise network services strategy utilizing the desktop environments.

Consider how widely technology – particularly the PC – is deployed in various ways throughout organizations and one can readily understand how difficult it is for an organization to bring its people together under a cohesive enterprise IS. The traditional corporate organization has crumbled and the workforce has dispersed. Users are transporting the PC onto planes and trains, into living rooms, customer sites, remote branch offices, and to other new frontiers. The result may be heightened individual and workgroup productivity, but overall business operation efficiency has not necessarily improved. In some cases, it may have even deteriorated.

Companies must focus on how to establish a strategic solution model for the corporate computing environment. This model should:

Support their operational, organizational, and technological evolution, and leverage existing multivendor systems and accommodate future growth

Improve the efficiency of business operations, allowing people to share information and corporate resources regardless of location and computing platform

Support a decentralized organization and centralized data and resources

Provide secure, reliable, and manageable enterprise communications

Increase profitability

This architectural model cannot be built using an applications strategy, a network operating system (NOS) strategy or an operating platform strategy. Experience dictates businesses need a well-defined strategy to incorporate these existing systems – one that combines the strategy paradigms and Internet/intranet technology. This approach must gauge current capabilities, forecast the near- and long-term future business needs, and prioritize what comes first in terms of business profitability.

In building a model for assessing the current needs and capabilities, one must consider the global scenario, the equipment inventory, the business decision process IT is supporting, the enterprise needs for security and availability, the IT objectives set for the current period and how to meet them, and how these issues will affect future needs.

International Logistics

As companies adopt a global business approach, IT managers must prepare for a new set of challenges. To graduate from multinational to global status, a company must change technical infrastructures and work processes. For many reasons, IT executives should develop a strategy and a governance structure that balances the needs of the enterprise as a whole with the needs of local units. There are many fundamental differences among locations that must be accommodated by IT services and products, including time zones, languages, regulatory environments, and basic technical infrastructures. A successful strategy accommodates these differences.

For supply logistics, many companies have tried a concept called "global sourcing," which involves centralized location and management for all IT purchasing. The positive aspect of this can be enhanced discounts, easier tracking of what already exists in the enterprise, and its depreciation by maintaining an asset database and centralized contract management for maintenance. The downside: This is a difficult job to master, especially if senior management does not buy-in to the concept. In this case, people may attempt to violate the system for smaller pieces of equipment such as PCs and printers, which would interfere with the IT asset tracking. This type of management position requires a great deal of persistence, negotiating expertise, and knowledge of all possible products and their usage.

One of the biggest challenges facing centralized IT logistics is the push and pull between centralized IT logistics management and local autonomy. It resembles the "80/20 rule," in that some – but not all – of the offices will adhere to the guidelines and send the requests through. The function of the global sourcing manager is a facilitator who speeds the coordination efforts versus a potential roadblock. It is helpful having local support contacts that managers can call – set-up via the centralized element – so the local office feels they have some control. This calling system, however, must be "policed" so designated individuals are calling, and not just anyone at that location.

A person who holds the global sourcing role must be an effective leader and team facilitator in the areas of sales and marketing, manufacturing, total quality control, and product development, in addition to outsourcing.

Global sourcing does not work for all organizational structures. There must be a centralized element in the regional structure to put the framework in place to make this position work. Coordination is the key to global sourcing, between regions and within the suppliers. Consider, for example, a company that buys both hardware and software from one of the major IT suppliers. Coordinating a global discount for purchase across product lines with the vendor is – in the IT timeline – still a fairly new concept and requires diligence on the part of the customer to ensure the discount is given correctly. Another problem is quality standards. IT managers may be forced to adopt global IT standards and purchasing contracts that do not meet local operating demands.

Managing the enterprise's IT assets is now more difficult than ever because managing C/S assets is far more complicated and costly than doing so in a legacy environment. In the centralized days, it was easy to count the number of dumb terminals linked to a mainframe. Today, it is a different matter because there are software packages, PCs, and workstations distributed to multiple worldwide servers. Locating and managing all the assets within a company's C/S infrastructure is the first and most critical step before managers can regain control.

Building an Asset Database

How does one build and maintain an asset database? The technology is available in terms of custom specific software packages, professional outsourcing assistance, and "do-it-yourself" database packages. How does one keep the database up-to-date after it is built? The technology can perform most of the maintenance, but from a management point of view, one must also have the local offices motivated to provide information. A recommendation is the "carrot and stick" approach, where a benefit/reward scheme keeps people providing the centralized source with information on local configurations, with some sort of penalty for not doing so. An example of this would be prioritizing who receives the new software releases. This can backfire, however, but in the case of corporate dealings positive reinforcement is better than negative nagging.

Another issue for international logistics is technical support and maintenance. One trend is providing internal customer support via the corporate intranet. Shifting the response center, using the regional structure (of most companies) to compensate for the time zone differences, the corporate intranet can be an advanced company bulletin board-type system where users can send their IT problems to be tracked and solved 24 hours a day. If a problem is not solved by one regional center, it can be passed along to the next time zone for a continuous approach to bug repairs and problem solving. Interoperability and responsiveness to customer needs becomes difficult if the resources are not continually accessible enterprisewide, in every department, and at all remote locations.

However, strategy and infrastructure only takes a business so far. To go the international distance, be prepared to travel. Many IT executives spend so much time on the road coordinating global IT activities, their home offices are constantly empty.

IT advances are at the heart of an enterprise's ability to adopt a global approach to business. With international responsibilities, IT executives can count on adding a new layer of complexity to their already demanding positions. There also are benefits, however. Because IT advances are key enablers to this dominant business trend, IT executives are in a position to create new global alliances, refine their entrepreneurial skills, and demonstrate to senior management they can deliver the services and products that drive global success.

Role of Legacy Equipment in an Interoperable Environment

The viability of legacy equipment such as minicomputers and mainframes in today's business environment is the subject of much discussion in the trade press. HP recently made headlines for unplugging its last mainframe. What role does "more mature" equipment have in the current technological phase in business? Does the company have to replace its technology with changes in its IT strategy? The answer is no. Combining legacy equipment and C/S offers the best of both worlds. Most IT managers pursue a phased-in migration strategy. The manner in which a company prioritizes applications for migration depends on the level of equipment and code investment the company has and the maintenance level necessary to maintain operational status.

Some organizations have "reinvented" the role of the mainframe, making it into a specialized applications server for applications such as manufacturing and administrative finance, where its power is useful. The current view of the mainframe can be summarized as an important part of the past and of the future, as shown in Figure 2.1. The minicomputer can also be harnessed as a workgroup server, again for special application areas where the code already exists.

Figure 2.1 What Are Your Mainframe Plans?

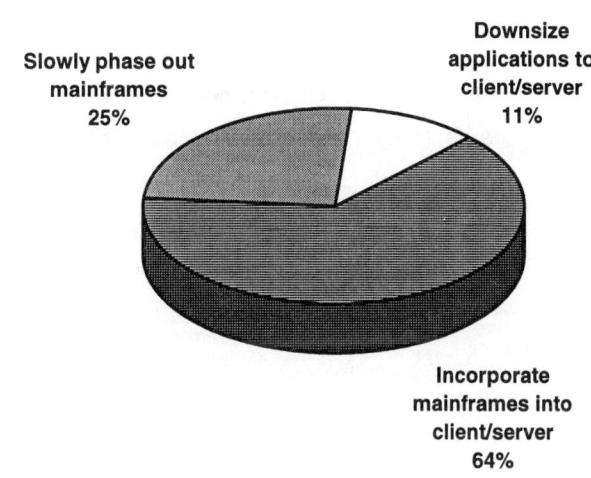

Slowly phase out mainframes 25%

Downsize applications to client/server 11%

Incorporate mainframes into client/server 64%

Source: Alliance Development Corp. survey of 100 IT Managers

Part of the reason for maintaining legacy applications in some revised form is the amount of investment already put into these systems. The conversion costs are sometimes prohibitive to move to new technology. Occasionally, new technology does not result in increased productivity with certain applications. The reason for migrating is not to reduce IT costs, but to improve organizational alignment. Invariably, C/S migration projects – especially those with significant custom application development phases – are more difficult, lengthy, and costly than expected.

If the company does want to move parts of the mainframe database such as financial or human resource records, then move the business functions to C/S because they are the applications that contribute to the corporation's bottomline. From a price/performance standpoint, internal functions such as human resources, payroll, accounts payable/receivable, and general ledger can be run more economically by leaving them on legacy systems because there are no strategic benefits from moving them to C/S. Actually, C/S has increased the demand for mainframes and other legacy systems, not reduced it. "Tried and true" technology is always needed to smooth the transition to enabling technology.

An Interoperable Organization

Many organizations today have stable and cost-effective IT platforms. Some of these platforms are aging, however, and will soon require attention. Often, an enterprise will continue with the choices that have served it well in the past. In some cases, maintaining existing technology infrastructures will be a satisfactory approach. Why? Because the perceived cost of the status quo is less than the perceived transition cost with its various cultural, financial, and organizational impacts.

There are compelling reasons for adopting an interoperable approach to computing environment. Users can extend flexibility to their operations, increase productivity, and reduce technology and conversion costs. The rise of the interoperability concept in the corporate computing arena is due to the manifold benefits of interconnecting computing equipment from a variety of manufacturers. Interoperable computing enables end-users to use almost any platform to perform productive work because they know their data can be combined with data and work performed on other platforms. Interoperability enables a much greater degree of resource-sharing and can help systems buyers make economical purchases based on the ability to buy from many different sources. Interoperable equipment is intended to increase productivity and eliminate the hidden costs of less effective computing systems.

How does one change the mentality of the enterprise to embrace the issues of interoperability? The evolution of organizational structures and cyberspace will yield to utterly new business models. Traditional corporations are structure-driven and their typical response to an outside threat or opportunity has been to reorganize. In contrast, a new environment should be relationship-driven, favoring formless internal structures and the ability to rapidly change external partnerships and alliances. Vendors are calling this the "extended enterprise," where suppliers and customers are part of the enterprise computing circle and connections to enterprise computing resources are needed. The extended enterprise is emerging due to business pressures to compete. Many companies are finding their direct competitors are also becoming their partners for certain projects, thus blurring the lines of business behaviors.

The corporate organization is likely to be affected by the Internet and the potential of electronic commerce. In particular, relationships between firms will be symbiotic. Organizations will be defined by relationships rather than organizational boundaries. Interlinked arrangements are expected to evolve. Internal corporate structures are changing, with flattened management hierarchies and redefined jobs. One of the trends affecting corporate structures is the move toward the combination of communications and computers.

In combining different communications and computing structures, the role of setting standards in an enterprise falls to the IT department. According to a recent report from Forrester Research, setting standards on a limited set of foundation technologies such as E-mail, financial systems, and transmission control protocol/Internet protocol (TCP/IP) networks strengthens infrastructure stability. However, applying excessive resources to enforce a multitude of corporate technology standards costs too much and consumes too much of the chief information officer (CIO) and IT department's valuable time. Corporations understand why foundation technology standards are enforced when it results in significant financial payback. Flexibility and responsiveness within an organization's IT department can be more important for organizational interoperability than a corporatewide infrastructure policy.

Another, perhaps more daunting organizational issue is staffing – at least from the management perspective. Innovative IT management requires staff members with keen technical skills. Today, there is an acute shortage of people qualified to perform certain critical tasks, especially areas such as SAP R/3 programming and Java programming. The growth of new networks and distributed systems has created enormous demand, and thus, a bidding war for the top professionals in this arena. Managers must contend with escalating salaries and a high turnover rate.

The highest hurdle for IT staff is going to be the overall change in orientation. Many IT professionals are still mainframe-centric in their thinking; C/S is different, as shown in Figure 2.2. It is a jump to change the way they think. The tools are skills they will learn. However, they will build applications that still resemble mainframe applications unless they change the way they think about C/S computing.

Figure 2.2 Skills Gap

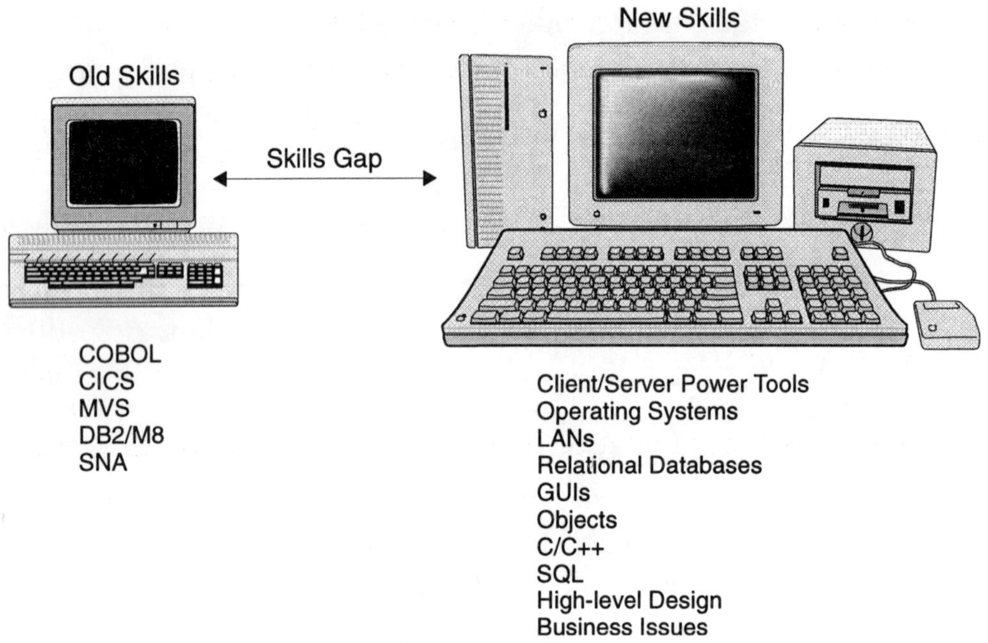

New Skills

Old Skills

Skills Gap

COBOL
CICS
MVS
DB2/M8
SNA

Client/Server Power Tools
Operating Systems
LANs
Relational Databases
GUIs
Objects
C/C++
SQL
High-level Design
Business Issues

If a manager is fortunate enough to build a stable organization for IT management, advances in technology will rapidly erode staff skills. Regular training is necessary so skills will not become obsolete. Training is the proverbial "thorn in the side" of every IT department. It is expensive and time consuming, and the benefits are difficult to measure. Despite these drawbacks, however, training is also absolutely essential to keep pace with ever-changing technology. Table 2.1 lists the types of issues involved in selecting training courses for IT staff.

Table 2.1 IT Training Issues

Key Point:
Assess a number of elements including cost, type of training, length of training program, the amount of people to be trained over time and expected results.

<u>Suggestions and Techniques:</u>

- The best way to find an adequate course is through personal recommendation.

- Consider the course outline, which should cover the course content, what the person should be able to do upon completing it, and the necessary prerequisite skills and qualifications.

- Consider any course critiques and evaluations published in any periodical.

- With a new supplier, just book one employee to take a course to test the quality of training and obtain feedback.

- Decide how important it is whether the course should lead to a professional qualification such as a certified network engineer (CNE) or Microsoft Certified Systems Engineer.

- For technical training, seek authorized training providers such as Microsoft Authorized Technical Education Centers (ATECs) or Novell Authorized Education Centers.

The IT manager who is responsible – generally the person resembling a hamster running on a wheel – exerts energy but never makes any real progress. It is little wonder many large organizations outsource many of the larger parts of the IT function.

What kind of person does such an IT organization require? Table 2.2 is a list of skills demonstrated by the ideal IT candidate, refined and developed from the Xerox Corporation rating suite of skills. Table 2.3 outlines the IT skills needed to cope in today's environment, defined by the IT Skills Forum.

Table 2.2 IT Manager's Wish List for a New IT Employee

Business Skills	Technical Skills	Management Skills
◆ Knowledge of the business, the market it participates in, and the economic influences involved	◆ Knowledge of current and past technology to an acceptable level for the structure internally and interested in how the technology can be better utilized ◆ Active in acquiring knowledge on the emerging technologies	◆ Knowledge of their own value to the organization ◆ Positive motivator ◆ Strategic thinker with tactical delivery ◆ Taker of calculated risks ◆ Communicates well at several levels of hierarchy ◆ Team player ◆ Decision maker with flexible objective setting

Table 2.3 The IT Skills Spectrum

Skill	Description
Visioning	The leadership ability of both technical and non-technical staff to imagine/visualize how new technology capabilities can be, and are, introduced for the benefit of the organization and its customers.
Managing IT investment	Awareness of cost/benefits analysis. Must account for "hidden" costs (maintenance, learning curves) and hidden benefits (competitive advantage) for IT; ability to engage in partnership with IT vendors to develop business solutions.
Managing information	The capacity to cope with and organize information, and to control, discriminate, interpret, and filter information flows.
Problem solving with IT	The ability to distill the essence of a pressing business problem and then solve it by the innovative use of IT.
Practical IT skills	The aptitude to apply IT solutions optimally and appropriately

Skill	Description
	to the task at hand.
Aligning business and IT	Appreciating the "big picture" and building on an understanding of the organization's business processes so specified IT requirements support business objectives.
Integrating IT solutions	Abilities and attributes for communicating effectively with colleagues, customers, and suppliers to ensure IT solutions are successfully incorporated into the business.
Following procedures	The ability to implement procedures effectively, including appreciating and subscribing to administrative procedures that preserve the integrity of the organization's information and IT assets.
Implementing systems	The ability to manage projects and provide technical resources required to maintain the organization's IT investment and provide the specified functionality.

Source: Definitions from the IT Skills Forum

Can an IT manager find an employee with all of these skills? More importantly, can an IT manager take a current employee and add to their current skill level? The answer is no and yes, respectively. The key to keeping and motivating IT employees is investing in their talent and skills. Many managers fear doing so because they feel the employee will then take their skills and leave, thus requiring more costly training of other employees. In reality, a satisfied employee is one who feels their skills and talent are compensated and appreciated.

Further, effective developers will need a broad understanding of business issues and a new mindset to leverage the technological strengths. If one cannot compensate financially to the best of the company's ability, training and education can assist in retaining the best and the brightest.

Business Benefits of Interoperability

The first signs of business benefits caused by this shift toward interoperability are already evident. Examples include auto makers, such as General Motor Corp., which require suppliers to link into enormous corporate electronic data interchange (EDI) networks coordinating the movement of parts and finished products. Once these links are made, one can find it difficult to tell where one company stops and another begins. A supplier building auto parts for a single client on an EDI-coordinated, just-in-time

(JIT) basis may be an independent corporation on paper, but its fate is tied to the customer as completely as any of the customer's corporate divisions.

The benefits of interoperable technologies, such as EDI for the selling organization, are also significant. One *Fortune* 100 technology company estimates face-to-face selling time could improve by as much as 40% by eliminating the involvement of its sales force in transactional "information gophering" for customers. By forming the appropriate relationships, companies will be better equipped to succeed on all fronts: Emerging markets, developing technologies, leveraging experience, and extending capital resources.

A lean IT interconnected organization is no longer enough. Businesses are coming to expect interoperability to provide high-value activities such as business and application architecture, which can build applications resilient to business change focusing on quality customer service and low cost.

To add this kind of value, IT must understand and anticipate its customers' needs (which include suppliers and external customers), and in particular, communicate how IT investments support the business' ability to change itself as conditions dictate. The IT department must think through the sources and implications of instability in the business environment, and educate business managers about how and where IT can help, with the CIO taking the lead.

Just as the enterprise must be able to proficiently adapt in a continuously changing business environment, the IT organization must be able to use interoperability to create and manage IT services as flexibly as the business demands.

The IT department must link the dynamic business requirements with more flexible IT enablers. Business and IT teams must work together to analyze where the business sees threats and opportunities, brainstorm high-level IT actions, and evaluate how those affect the threats and opportunities. The most effective IT actions can be refined into actions in six areas over which a CIO has some measure of control:

1. Technology usage

2. Services

3. Organization

4. Operations

5. Standards and other electronic data processing (EDP) policies

6. Technology processes

The result is a set of detailed priorities that directly link back to business requirements.

Interoperability Decisions Impacting IT Objectives

Interoperability in the enterprise requires a sound methodology transforming new and enabling technology into quickly responsive IT services. A management program is also needed to ensure both long- and short-term results are achieved. For many IT organizations, ensuring results means moving away from a project-oriented approach to a process-oriented approach aimed at building and refreshing a shared infrastructure and also offering basic and customized services. Today's IT technical staff are increasingly developing extra skills and combining their specialist knowledge with management issues to fully maximize IT potential.

Meeting business objectives and managing user expectations has often been interpreted by IT staff as how to keep users quiet. Users are not often given what they need, but only what IT can provide and therefore the users are not satisfied. The difficulties include actually capturing requirements in the operational environment.

Accurately capturing user requirements is no easy task. IT managers confirm users often decide they need a specific technology because they have read about it in a magazine, for example. Unless their requirements are quickly clarified, they will also change their minds about what they need during the project. This often happens as new business needs emerge.

Conflicts between IT departments and end-users over which suppliers to use may also arise because both end-users and the IT department have their preferred suppliers. Then political campaigning occurs, usually to the board level. Finally, lack of knowledge and understanding feeds into technological differences such as not understanding compatibility or support issues.

This extension of user requirements into external resource issues is one symptom of a corporate environment which encourages competition for internal business on an open market.

A fundamental problem: In many cases, the members of the technical staff are not trained educators. Despite this problem, a large part of the job involves communicating and educating users and management to obtain approval for projects. For each project, the IT manager must have a comprehensive explanation of how it will match the company's business objectives. IT managers must gain the full support of business unit management to make their project a success. Training and education external to the company can be of assistance in doing one's job in this case.

Decision Drivers

The major IT drivers for changes affecting business objectives, not surprisingly, are the shift to new architectures, the explosion of the Internet and corporate intranets, and the deployment of C/S technology. Because of technology shifts, the recent increases in long-term spending for IT are no longer cyclical. C/S technology and the Internet/intranets will keep overall spending plans around current rates for the near future. The industry is entering a renewed cycle in desktop hardware and software with the adoption of 32-bit operating systems, which will also increase C/S advances. Because most user implementation efforts began in the mid-1990s, full implementation – which takes roughly three to four years – will last through the turn of the century.

A 1994 *Information Week* survey of almost 200 IT executives revealed individual business units and corporate IT departments take part in C/S purchases. The findings parallel 1993 results which also revealed a move toward a joint partnership in decision making. The 1994 survey findings demonstrated three in four respondents indicated their firms will increase spending on C/S systems in the next calendar year. (At this writing a more recent survey had not been published by *Information Week*.) Findings also demonstrated IT has permeated all functions and levels of firms. Industry analysts suggest business unit users and managers are influencing IT decisions because they bring in revenue.

Transition Strategies

How does a company move toward a more dynamic, interoperable environment from a static and centralized one? Many companies have been trying with C/S technology, and paying the penalties for their lack of foresight. Going overboard with change is a certain recipe for failure. Change is feared by many, but some organizations deal with it better than others. Tables 2.4 lists the key points in preparing for an IT transition strategy.

Table 2.4 IT Transition Strategy Components

Start small – Try a sample operation area or application to move first. Find a business unit with a willing and flexible "champion" who supports change.

Start with a non-critical, but visible area – Usually a sales or marketing operation is one of the best areas to start, because it is highly visible but does not affect mission-critical areas such as payroll or manufacturing. By selecting an application area that "sells" the changes proposed for the rest of the organization, the focus will be on the way the current business process works and how it should work in the future.

Understand the business and the desired results, rather than allowing technology to run the business – It is important to build consensus, commitment, and organizational structure early on to support the changes.

Have a realistic time frame and outcome – Be conservative about the time frame because an early completion will be a pleasant surprise. Plan the necessary outcome to move more areas of the operation down the path of change. Show measurable and solid results.

Teamwork works – Designate a project team and train the team in each of the particular phases on which they are going to work. The training involves more than the tools, it also involves altering the development mind-set to new ideas and technologies.

Transition success goes beyond organization and training – Many functions must be incorporated into new developments to maximize developer productivity and facilitate the creation of robust applications.

The architectural framework is a key element for success – Use a deployment architecture that enables a multi-tier structure. Application partitioning and transaction support are important for new applications because they improve performance, reduce database-licensing costs, and allow distributed applications and databases to be created.

Plan for change management issues to arise – Be prepared and plan for the business and IT operational changes and new relationships the technology will bring into the work environment.

There are obviously more techniques involved for transition, but each political situation is different. Change management – which is what any transition is – must be carefully assessed before, during, and after any changes are made, both for business purposes and organizational stability. Keep in mind the focus should be on how to provide more effective business processes and applications enabling business management to vault onto new business opportunities.

Security in a Hierarchical Environment

Security is always a popular topic. Without built-in network security, the global network cannot play a role in business. How many companies are currently using the Internet/intranet technology for confidential, mission-critical operations? Very few.

Proprietary security solutions are currently standard. They are, however, difficult to integrate across the enterprise. An effective enterprise security service must provide connections between multiple security schemes in different environments. Managers responsible for securing enterprise networks have expressed their fears over the ever-increasing ways in which their distributed computing environments can be compromised.

Although mainframes and centralized applications will continue for some time, most network managers will also have to contend with the onslaught of C/S technologies. The advent of mobile computing has also raised a new set of security issues. Securing the new array of systems is critical to the business advantage IT provides. Distributed enterprise networks are relatively vulnerable – compared with mainframe systems that preceded them – and security is rapidly becoming a main business priority.

As companies complete security product installation, they must first establish enterprisewide security policies and enforce them across all platforms. They should, for example, establish policies regarding PC use, which involves changing the way they view PCs. As corporate assets, today's PCs are critical to companies because they contain valuable information, are more widely accessible than older technology, and are as necessary as a basic appliance such as a telephone or a calculator.

Many IT professionals debate whether users can be trusted with critical data because most desktop functions are important to the enterprise's stability. PCs have flourished because of increased ease-of-use and user access to software applications and hardware. Companies should be careful because the PC is an extension of its user and the information that is placed on the server from the machine should be measured.

Managers can ensure PCs and LANs are more secure by making PCs an extension of the enterprise instead of the user, and by using encryption and authentication programs which can identify "trusted clients" within the enterprise.

Network security products for the distributed environment continue to evolve and advance, offering more protection than previously available. Because numerous products are available, selecting the most appropriate ones can be time consuming. Security products, as with other types of equipment, must be evaluated not just for their security functions, but also for their ease-of-use and manageability. IT managers must understand three main components of enterprise network security: Authentication, authorization, and encryption. Authentication allows administrators to use tools such as passwords to prevent access. A safer alternative uses intelligent tokens to generate one-time-only passwords authenticated by a secure server. Authorization allows an administrator to have authority over who can access certain resources on the network. Encryption guarantees information being transmitted across a network can only be read or replaced by authorized users.

Administering C/S security systems demands a high level of technical skill because they are complex applications. Some users in large corporations with varied environments can have various sign-ons and passwords. Mainframe security packages cannot be expanded to smaller processors and these security complexities will continue to increase as companies store more crucial information on C/S systems. Single sign-on (SSO) systems and common user identifications (IDs) have not been successful for enterprise systems. These systems are composed of multiple servers at many levels, each requiring user log-ons.

Managers must also remember to spend time educating end-users. One technique is to use current events to remind everyone about security issues. For example, when a virus is found in the company, tell people about it. When an article appears in the newspaper, share it with other employees.

Other possible protective measures include physical security for servers, anti-virus software scans, daily log-on reports, easy-to-use scanning methods for foreign floppy disks, user authentication tools that require password changes, and encrypted transmission of passwords. The bottomline: Training is the least expensive and easiest preventive measure within the enterprise.

Chapter 3

Hardware Platforms and Portability

At the core of the interoperability challenge is the hardware platform, complete with its various choices of processors. Toward the end of this decade, it is likely users will be able to purchase any combination of hardware platform and operating system (OS) they want, rather than being concerned with selecting the best UNIX-reduced instruction set computer (RISC) server or the optimal Intel PC server. The selections will include hardware based on Intel chips, Sun Microsystems' SPARC chips, MIPS Technologies' chips, DEC's Alpha chips, and IBM/Motorola/Apple PowerPC chips. System vendors also will offer different choices for operating systems. Even IBM plans to factory-load OS/2, Advanced Interactive Executive (AIX) UNIX or Sun's Solaris on PowerPC workstations. Users may be initially confused as they try to determine the best combination of OS and platform, but there will be a variety of advantages. First, it will be easy to install a hardware platform and change applications to reflect business conditions. Desktop hardware – particularly PCs – are at the commodity phase, much like other office equipment where the brand name and its marketing perception may be the only difference between the platforms.

For most companies, applications software is the driving force behind the establishment of a corporate hardware platform policy. According to company representatives at the Client/Server Summit (sponsored by *Computer Reseller News* and held in December 1995 in New York), standardization around the C/S architecture is expected to provide a measure of interoperability for software products. A continuing difficulty with product standardization is that vendors are reluctant to adopt their products to a lowest common denominator. The vendors feel value is added by incorporating proprietary features and functions. Another difficulty: Standardized products are often incapable of meeting the rigorous demands of mission-critical systems. As a result, many database vendors find themselves testing products with an agenda of 40 or 50 different platforms in mind. A representative of Sybase, Inc., noted Sybase tests approximately 2,500 different hardware and software configurations. The testing problem is passed on to the computer systems integration channel, causing some vendors to call for the funding of an Underwriter's Laboratory equivalent to handle system testing.

Controlling Systems Management

With a wide variety of system platforms in the enterprise, companies have several choices on how to manage the systems: In-house expertise, outsourcing to one or many IT consultants or turning to the vendors for support. Management and maintenance of distributed systems environment with remote workgroups, networks, and other resources necessary for C/S computing is a complex business, requiring a necessary investment of time and personnel. According to recent industry surveys, staying abreast of IT equipment is a worthwhile endeavor because it consumes about 7% or 8% of hardware costs.

Companies lacking the finances to staff an in-house team will need to choose between vendor- or third-party-supplied maintenance. Most hardware platforms include a one year warranty. Vendors will offer an extension on the warranty, under which maintenance is offered at a reduced rate. If a third-party provider is the option chosen, third-party maintenance providers should be hired on the basis of their ability to maintain particular equipment. A provider's success can usually be measured by checking its reference list. Most providers offer a host of flexible time and coverage options, ranging from 24-hours a day, seven-days a week; or time and materials per incident, but the company should get a promise of response time for all contracts; a customer of a third-party service provider should have assurances of response time. If the third-party provider cannot make the repairs and the vendor must be called in, the customer should be reimbursed. Because the cost of downtime can far exceed the maintenance cost, keeping up with IT equipment maintenance is worth the time and money.

For a company that can justify an in-house service organization and an inventory of spare parts, maintenance is not a problem. Some companies, however, do not want IT as their core competency, and obtain maintenance through a contract with a vendor or a third-party provider. In complex, multivendor environments, a maintenance vendor for one piece of equipment may not help with the attached peripherals and other hardware. The complex IT environment becomes part of a complex business relationship. Companies need IT staff – whether internal or external – that understand the environment. Hardware platform acquisition, maintenance, and service should be treated as a combined business decision.

Operating Systems: Supporting Mixed-Platform Client/Server Environments

An increasing number of operating systems support mixed-platform C/S environments, an example of which is Microsoft's intention to integrate its Windows NT 3.5 OS with NetWare and UNIX. Focus is shifting from the OS to applications because users want to run their applications anywhere, regardless of the method used. In that light, operating systems are becoming vehicles to execute applications. IBM, Microsoft, Novell, and various UNIX vendors are vying for dominance in the C/S OS market; some operating systems are gravitating toward the client – Windows, for example – while others are moving toward the server. Some operating systems such as Windows NT 3.5 are moving toward both. In Figure 3.1, the global growth of C/S-oriented operating systems is shown, with an emphasis on NT and UNIX.

Figure 3.1 Client/Server Operating System Growth

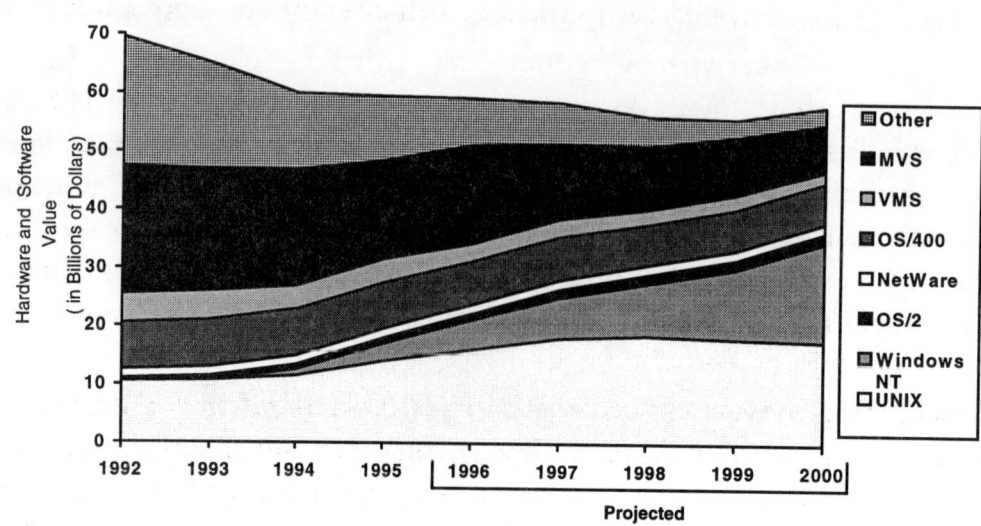

Source: EITO/Gartner Group

Though they would to prefer to stay with one OS, many firms find themselves running an increasingly pluralistic blend. Vendor efforts to integrate help the situation because users want to run their applications anywhere, regardless of location.

OS vendors, notoriously territorial – including the "open" vendors – are working to create a C/S world that has fewer borders. While they are not putting aside all of their differences to achieve co-existence in this new heterogeneous terrain, they are talking détente.

Through support for various standards efforts, APIs, and each other's networking protocols, OS vendors are making it easier for users to create varied platform – C/S environments. At the same time, OS vendors are working toward integration, as the focus is moving from the OS to applications. Users are interested in application availability; they are unconcerned with how it got there. They want to buy their application shrink-wrapped and run it anywhere.

Still, the majority of management information systems (MIS) shops, given the choice, would opt for a homogeneous OS environment because of system and network administration concerns. According to D.H. Brown Associates, a leading research analysis firm in New York, research has shown that customers will always prefer to purchase their solutions from a single vendor.

The reality, though, is a world in which end-users and departmental managers often make technological decisions independently from MIS. It is also a world where mergers and acquisitions frequently bring together disparate computing environments. The result: Pluralism. A company must be open to the possibility of utilizing multiple operating systems. The MIS job is to ensure they are buying a viable solution that serves user needs.

Will operating systems ever be portable across hardware platforms, and do users really care? In an X/Open Market Research Report, respondents ranked portable operating systems as the most important systems technology for supporting business functions. However, the report noted, "Portable operating systems are valued less for their ability to run on a variety of hardware platforms and more for their ability to run applications on those hardware systems."

Along the same line as the X/Open report, a study of nearly 100 IT managers by Alliance Development Corporation in Phoenix showed 30% of the managers attributed the upswing in the mainframe market to the belief that some mainframe applications simply cannot run on other platforms. Portability may be more feasible, but the mind set of industry is to focus on the application and its development.

Users believe OS vendors have an obligation to create an open product and provide the transports for application and database management system (DBMS) portability. The market would rather see less concern about whose version of UNIX is being utilized and more concern with interoperability issues – making working together the real issue. DCE from the OSF of Cambridge, Massachusetts is a strong effort in that direction, but making interoperability the focus may take some time. The task is more complex than putting an OS on a machine. There are different speeds of machines, interconnects, and many differences within the operating systems.

IBM is leading an effort to establish a common-agent technology standard for OS interoperability based on simple network management protocol (SNMP) and desktop management interface (DMI) specifications. The common agent is composed of a DMI service layer, a mapping layer for DMI to SNMP conversion, and interfaces for reconfiguring altered SNMP and multiplexing SNMP traffic. Under the system, SNMP-based management systems will have a DMI-compliant server, software, workstation, and component management capability. The number of agents operating on managed resources will be reduced under the system, cutting network management expense. However, concern exists over the agent's inability to recognize remote procedure call (RPC) or common management interface protocol (CMIP) protocol-based agents. IBM's close work with the Desktop Management Task Force (DMTF) bodes well for the agent's compatibility with the committee's final mapping standard. This parallels other work in this area, where efforts are under way to reduce the expenses and resources necessary to maintain OS interoperability.

Processors and Portability – RISC and Intel

The apparent winners of the overall processor wars are the RISC architectures for advanced computing needs and Intel processors for both parallel processing and desktop architectures. From a processor standpoint, however, interoperability is more than chip matching. Intel's dominance in the microprocessor industry is based on the de facto application binary interface (ABI) created by Intel and Microsoft, but this could decline as emulation replaces the need for specific microprocessors or operating systems. It may be a couple of years before emulation is perfected, but it should soon be simple to emulate Windows applications on other microprocessors.

If the company is struggling with the Intel versus RISC dilemma, start with applications requirements, not with the chip architecture. If the 32-bit necessary applications are available on Intel's Pentium Pro, wait for the appropriate servers to become available. Next, examine OS requirements in the form of Windows NT versus the UNIX OS. If users are demanding NT, the main choices are Pentium-based servers or DEC's Alpha.

Because of the relative lack of scalability of Intel's Pentium Pro systems and supported operating systems, Pentium Pro servers are expected to have the most impact at the lower end of enterprise applications. According to Dataquest, a market research firm in San Jose, California, the Pentium Pro will mostly likely "make significant headway in the lower one-third of the enterprise, but it remains to be seen whether these systems will be able to handle extremely large and complex databases."

If there is a near-term requirement to scale beyond the performance offered by Pentium Pro servers currently limited to four-way architectures, the company may be better off with RISC-UNIX combination which scales beyond 16 processors. Windows NT, on the other hand, is effectively limited to four-way symmetric multiprocessing (SMP). RISC servers running proprietary implementations of UNIX have preferred maintainability and availability because they can be clustered. For example, clustering for Pentium Pro servers running Windows NT will be available when version 4.0 is introduced.

For Windows NT users, RISC servers are losing whatever appeal they might have had. Gartner Group, a U.S. market research company advises if plans are to run NT, consider RISC only if there is a need for the highest performance box for specific tasks, such as high-end databases, rendering or digital pre-press, advises. Noting DEC argues its most recent Alpha implementation beats Pentium Pro in price/performance, Gartner replies: "the price/performance of a Ferrari is pretty good, too, but Ferraris are awfully expensive for day-to-day driving."

The 64-bit Question

Desktop users are now accustomed to the 16-bit architecture for office automation usage, including the 16-bit standard OS of MS-DOS and associated applications. Current architectural system standards are at the 32-bit level for most workstations and server systems. The recent trend toward 64-bit architecture is based on the need to optimally run enterprise databases and graphics applications on multiprocessor servers. The 64-bit architectures and associated operating systems will play an essential part in increasing response times and handling increasing volumes of transaction data. The number of 64-bit operating systems is expected to increase as more 64-bit microprocessors hit the market.

Just as the corporate world begins to invest in 32-bit operating systems, DEC, Microsoft, and others are working on 64-bit operating systems that leverage the horsepower of today's high-end workstations and servers.

Although many operating systems are currently 32-bit – including IBM OS/2 Warp, Microsoft Windows 95, Windows NT, and Mac – the market has shown interest in 64-bit operating systems. For example, IBM's OS/400, DEC's UNIX, and Silicon Graphics, Inc.'s (SGI's) Irix UNIX are all 64-bit operating systems. A 64-bit OS is necessary for a workstation to realize the potential of a 64-bit central processing unit (CPU) architecture because highly complex applications need more data space than the 4.2 gigabyte (GB) supported by 32-bit operating systems.

The number of 64-bit microprocessors on the market is also increasing. Products such as HP's PA-8000, SGI's R1000, DEC's Alpha 21164, and Sun Microsystems' UltraSparc will result in the release of more 64-bit operating systems. DEC recently released OpenVMS 7.0, a 64-bit version of virtual memory system (VMS) designed to run smoothly with its 64-bit Alpha hardware. In addition, HP is developing a 64-bit version of UNIX, Microsoft is working on a 64-bit version of Windows NT, and IBM is considering a 64-bit version of OS/2.

According to International Data Corp., a research firm in Framingham, Massachusetts, "it is inevitable that software developers and companies will move to 64-bit environments" given the hardware improvements. Consider DEC's OpenVMS 7.0 which includes a new file system – called Spiralog – developed at the University of California at Berkeley. DEC says Spiralog improves capacity and performance of online data backup in C/S environments.

Oracle is among the software vendors trying to exploit OpenVMS 7.0 and its 64-bit basis. The database giant, which purchased DEC's relational database software, Rdb, released a new version of Oracle Rdb 7 optimized for 64-bit performance on OpenVMS 7.0. Oracle already offers a 64-bit database for DEC UNIX.

Other 64-bit operating systems are on the way. HP is developing a 64-bit version of UNIX for a forthcoming 64-bit chip jointly designed by HP and Intel. Likewise, Microsoft insiders say the software giant is preparing a 64-bit version of Windows NT, though it will not arrive until 1998 at the earliest.

Attempting to keep pace, IBM is exploring the feasibility of a 64-bit version of OS/2 Warp. According to IBM, the OS could easily be upgraded to a 64-bit architecture by adding the IBM Microkernel to Warp. Warp for the PowerPC will ride the IBM Microkernel in 1996; Warp for Intel is slated to gain the microkernel in late 1996 or early 1997. IBM earlier converted OS/2 from 16 bits to 32 bits.

While promising and powerful, analysts say 64-bit operating systems will not escape niche status anytime soon. Most applications do not take advantage of 64-bit operating systems or hardware. The 64-bit architectures figure in long-term user plans, but it is not currently a "must-have." Software and hardware vendors, however, are clearly striving to change this situation.

By the year 2000, 64-bit chips will become the norm. "The move to 64-bit processing is as inevitable as night following day," says Mike Lambert, vice president of technical strategy with X/Open, the independent standards organization in Menlo Park, California. Are the 64 bits worth the associated migration headaches – applications must be rewritten or recompiled to reap maximum benefit – and the extra cost? If sales of DEC's 64-bit Alpha chip are any indication, a growing number of users think 64 bits are worth the trouble. In fact, DEC's Alpha business grew by 77% in fiscal year 1995.

Experts say two factors are driving 64-bit technology: Graphics-intensive computing and the need for heavy-duty databases. Typical examples include pharmaceutical giant SmithKline Beecham of Philadelphia that is tapping Alpha systems to store and analyze data in an application that involves simulating molecules, and Pratt & Whitney of East Hartford, Connecticut has deployed a cluster of Alphas for jet-engine design.

The *Milwaukee Journal/Sentinel* chose two Alpha-based servers to replace two Unisys V-380 "light" mainframes. Peter Stockhausen, the newspaper's IT vice president, says his company also looked at IBM's AS/400 minicomputer and an HP midrange system. "The HP and IBM were fairly comparable," he says. "DEC was significantly faster in total throughput." The *Journal/Sentinel* now runs its customer service database and billing system on the Alpha servers. Bottomline benefits include faster access to customer records and better customer service.

A major advantage these new chips offer: 64-bit computing breaks through the 4 GB memory limit of 32-bit systems. DEC's Alpha Server 8000, for instance, supports 14 GB of memory. The larger cache makes it possible to process enormous chunks of data on a single chip. "With 64 bits, one can have a large application running in memory," says Patrick Smyth, director of marketing with DEC's UNIX business segment in Maynard, Massachusetts. "That translates into dramatically improved performance and much shorter response times," he added.

Another technical barrier obliterated by a 64-bit architecture is file size. A 64-bit file system can handle much larger files than a 32-bit system – a decided advantage as images and video become part of a file system. Sheer speed is the most talked-about advantage of a 64-bit world. Chipmakers are already staking claims of possessing world-leading performance. Experts warn users not to get caught up in the benchmark hype. Technology managers should try before they buy. Regardless of the processor, however, it is fair to expect a major performance improvement when channeling an existing application through a 64-bit machine. A typical example: HP says 32-bit applications will run 70% to 100% faster on its PA-8000.

For most organizations, there is no need to rush into 64-bit computing. Fewer than 5% of current HP systems ship with the maximum 4 GB of memory, evidence of untapped potential on 32-bit systems. The extra power of 64-bit processors, is mainly needed for high-end database applications. For an application such as decision support, it is worth paying for the large memory because some benefit can be seen.

Graphics-intensive computing is the other strength of 64-bit chips, making them a good match for the real-time multimedia applications soon to appear on the World Wide Web (the Web). However, PowerPC partners IBM and Motorola, and PC chip giant Intel agree with HP's analysis that 32-bit chips will continue to meet the needs of most users. In fact, the 32-bit PowerPC 604 is nearly as powerful as the 64-bit PowerPC 620.

This dilemma has caused IBM and Motorola to delay the 620's release until mid-1997. They hope to widen the performance gap between the two processors by 1997. Intel and HP are partnering on a 64-bit architecture that combines the two dominant chip technologies: RISC and complex instruction set computing (CISC). The partners have yet to announce a microprocessor based on the HP-Intel Architecture, but experts expect a 64-bit chip – called the P7 – in 1997 or later. Until then, Intel will be pushing the Pentium Pro, a 32-bit processor released in 1995.

Long-term planners have their sights set on the new generation of 64-bit chips. The move toward 64-bit file systems and 64-bit processing are just stages in the IT evolution. It is important to recognize this and not develop 64-bit solutions insufficient for 128-bit and the more long-term picture.

Future of Windows and Windows NT Environments

From the MIS manager point of view, one might say Windows is a necessary evil. The domination of Microsoft on the desktop – both in the OS and office automation application markets – has pushed users to demand more memory and more speed out of their systems. With the increasing user needs driving the additional hardware and software purchases, IBM Corp., Microsoft, Novell, and a variety of UNIX vendors are competing for dominance as a C/S operating system provider. As the market matures, certain operating systems are gravitating toward the client side, while others are moving toward the server. Windows is often found at the client side and rarely at the server side. While one sees NT at both the client and server, it is seen more at the server and less at the client. There once was a great deal of OS/2 at the server, less at the client. Now, however, the market is starting to see a demand for OS/2 Warp at the client side.

UNIX is rarely run on the client side, except in emulation form. However, it is proliferating at the server level. UNIX vendors are pushing the OS for what they are calling an application server. While the term "application server" is new, it is the role UNIX has traditionally played. With the acquisition of UNIX System Laboratories, Novell inherited the core technology for UNIX System V, renamed UNIXWare. The role of the UNIX platform was generally used in business application-like environments, running a strategic application. In that sense it was always an application server. UNIXWare runs on Intel platforms, giving it a unique place in the world of the desktop server.

IBM's AIX, Sun's Solaris, and Microsoft NT are strong contenders to support C/S requirements in the near term. They have strong networking capabilities and support other components such as object technology. DEC is a strong supporter of NT on their Alpha systems, with the Alpha systems able to run both VMS and NT.

Although it is possible to have a number of integrated solutions, users tend to purchase as much from one supplier to keep their systems as homogeneous as possible. Users seek homogeneous environments for several reasons: One-stop shopping, LAN administration issues, and the software development environment. Functionality integration is a key issue when making the purchasing decisions.

For those companies successfully integrating heterogeneous networks and operating systems, system administration is a concern. For example, the Consumers Warehouse Center in Holbrook, New York has successfully connected an AppleTalk network to an IBM LAN Server 4.0 network which are both connected to a virtual address extension (VAX) clone host, but they find Mac file restoration problematic. The firm chose IBM LAN Server 4.0 over Novell and Microsoft NT for its robustness as a server and ease-of-use. The company still had to devise its own solution for restoration of Mac files, however.

The vendors working on the PowerPC effort are coming closer to solving the portability problem, but have not yet arrived at a solution. Compatibility can be based on a processor architecture, but it ties one down to a single architecture. The future lies with the software. As a result, battling for architectural standards is not so important overall.

The rejuvenation of platform independence lies with objects, which is truly interoperability at its best. Portability today is a forklift; users recompile code from application to application. An object can execute on the platform where it is located. While future usage is uncertain, users must factor long-term viability into its OS choices. By choosing Windows and Microsoft, users will be well-positioned for the object world with the Microsoft OLE standard, even if it is not identical to Common Object Request Broker Architecture (CORBA), a competing object standard from the Object Management Group (OMG) of Framingham, Massachusetts. The object development vendors are at least allowing for OLE 2.0 so users will not be the ones to lose out in the race.

As for Windows NT, the issue is still out for debate. DEC estimates that 10% to 15% of its global systems business is based on Windows NT and this growth is expected to continue at a healthy rate. In terms of hardware infrastructure, however, businesses may not be ready yet for NT servers alone.

NetWare Management

In addition to the management of C/S operating systems, add network operating systems to the mix: IBM LAN Server ran on top of OS/2, NT Server is embedded in Microsoft LAN Manager, Banyan is sitting on top of UNIX, and Novell NetWare is within itself. OS interoperability is not the issue, rather what is required is system interoperability, which includes the OS, communications software, networking software, and file system.

Vendors have addressed many of the network integration issues with recent versions. Yet, the preferred enterprisewide platform of the 1990s must support the major PC and Mac networking protocols, TCP/IP for UNIX, and Internet access. The majority of the PC market uses Novell, Inc.'s NetWare for local-area networking and all UNIX vendors should support NetWare protocols with their products. Microsoft has adopted this approach with Windows NT and Windows 95, supporting NetWare protocols and providing client access to NetWare file and print servers. In 1995, NetWare's market share was estimated at 20 million nodes, too large a presence for UNIX vendors to ignore. Some UNIX vendors are offering add-ons to provide NetWare connectivity.

Novell's OS strategy is to create a super network operating system (SuperNOS) microkernel in UNIXWare 3.0 that will share common code with NetWare. In 1995, UNIXWare and NetWare established common SMP interfaces and support Open Datalink Interface (ODI), NetWare's proprietary IPX/SPX protocol, and the TCP/IP protocol. UNIXWare 2.0 includes a single log-in and bidirectional print capability between UNIXWare and NetWare networks.

Large companies are at a turning point. The current market situation and future prospects have caused many network planners to step back and take a hard look at the future. To give them further pause, Microsoft Windows NT has been touting advanced network services. Users are asking: With networking services embedded in NT, do I even need NetWare?

LAN internetworks have become critical corporate highways, but IT departments are facing shrinking support budgets and staff reductions. As a result, users look to their LAN OS to incorporate both systems management and a global network view, as shown in Figure 3.2. According to research conducted by Forrester Research (a U.S. market research firm), companies relying on large networks with hundreds of servers and thousands of desktops want centralized, remote administration - not technicians upgrading software and performing backups.

This management demand is a door opener for Windows NT. Among Forrester Research's corporate research sampling what companies required currently of their LAN operating systems, 41% of those considering NT cite Microsoft's systems management application as a factor. Microsoft also addressed NetWare integration in NT 3.5 and improved support for TCP/IP.

Figure 3.2 Systems Management and a Global Network View

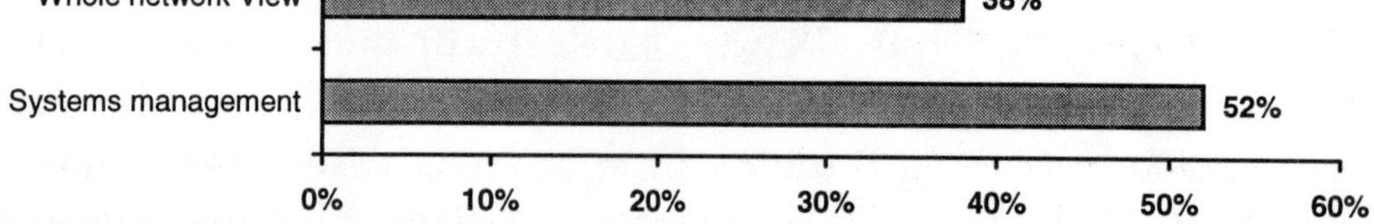

Source: Forrester Research, Inc.

Microsoft offers a variety of NetWare connectivity services in Windows NT Workstation and Windows NT Server. The Client Service for NetWare allows the Windows NT workstation to connect to the file and print services provided by NetWare servers. The Gateway service for NetWare provides networked and remote users connected to Windows NT server access to the file storage and printer resources on NetWare servers. With NWLink, the internetwork packet exchange/sequenced packet exchange (IPX/SPX)-compatible transport that comes with NT workstation and server, NetWare clients can access server applications such as Microsoft structured query language (SQL) server, system network architecture (SNA) server, and others running on Windows NT server without changing the client.

Fielding a good application server means assembling a very different package than that required by an adequate "file and print" server. Windows NT is a general-purpose OS and therefore offers some of the comfort NetWare lacks: Virtual memory, threads, portability to other processors, a single, familiar API for both client and server applications, and strong application development tools.

Windows NT also addresses some of the scalability issues that limited NetWare 3.x. It runs on processors such as Alpha, MIPS, PowerPC, and Intel, and it runs on SMP configurations of up to 32 processors.

Windows NT's extra features are available at a cost. In general, it requires more and better hardware than its competition to perform well. Given the inexpensive price of hardware and the small fraction of the overall lifetime ownership costs it represents, purchasing larger, faster hardware is a simple way of handling that objection. Windows NT clearly lags behind NetWare 4.1 in directory services.

Because NetWare 4.1 and Windows NT field such complementary strengths, many enterprises are finding their best path lies in combining the two. Tools from Microsoft such as Client Service for NetWare or Gateway Service for NetWare allow Windows NT clients to access file and print services on NetWare servers. Microsoft's File and Print Service for NetWare runs on an NT server, making NetWare clients resemble a NetWare 3 server.

What is the interoperable answer for NOS? When Microsoft and Novell come to a long-lasting agreement, the real answer will emerge. In the meantime, however, NetWare is the basis for many corporate workgroups with Microsoft applications layered on top. The mixture is starting to show fruition in examples such as Windows 95 Service Pack 1, which will include a NetWare 4.1 client.

What Is on the Desktop?

Until recently, there has been a distinct line drawn between PCs and workstations. Workstations represented powerful processor performance and industrial strength applications, while the PC stood for cost-efficient personal productivity applications and tools. The boundaries are now being erased as high-performance and high-volume processors have brought the power of the workstation to the PC price-point, and in many cases, to the PC itself.

A company's ability to do business effectively and competitively is affected by the openness and scalability of its IT strategy. Therefore, the desktop platform choice, focusing on such issues as cost of ownership and flexibility of resources, should reflect the company's desire to provide the most open environment to achieve business benefits from its use of technology.

The PC is a computing platform in transition. For the past decade, the desktop PC has primarily been a tool for personal productivity. Now that the corporate world is embracing C/S, the role of the PC is set to evolve.

The days of the PC as a pure personal productivity tool are numbered. Historically, the vast majority of corporate PCs were used to share files, run spreadsheets or send E-mail. When users need access to business systems, they connect to mainframes and minicomputers via terminal emulation. However, the connection mode has changed. PC users are working in C/S mode for business applications. In addition, terminal emulation will decline and evolve to a more specialist niche of graphics and multimedia terminals.

To support the PC's new role, desktop hardware will also need to evolve. In the last few years, the average desktop relied on a 486 processor and 14 MB of memory, up from a 386 with 6 MB to 8 MB of memory. If one should want TCP/IP, Novell, and Windows all on one machine, 12 MB of memory is the recommended minimum.

Why do PCs need more power? Simply put, the C/S "charge" is activated. A majority of large companies are now actively involved in building and running C/S systems. As users think of PCs as delivery vehicles for business-critical programs, their shopping lists – for both technology features and vendor characteristics – are being revised. On the technology side, users insist on connectivity options and multitasking. Vendors, meanwhile, are expected to deliver the perfect combination of reliability, service, and low prices. Also, changes in networks and software applications have placed strong demands for investment in new PC systems and servers. Figure 3.3 shows IDC's research of 300 top European IT executives and their business needs for investing in PC server technology.

Figure 3.3 Business Case for PC Server Investment

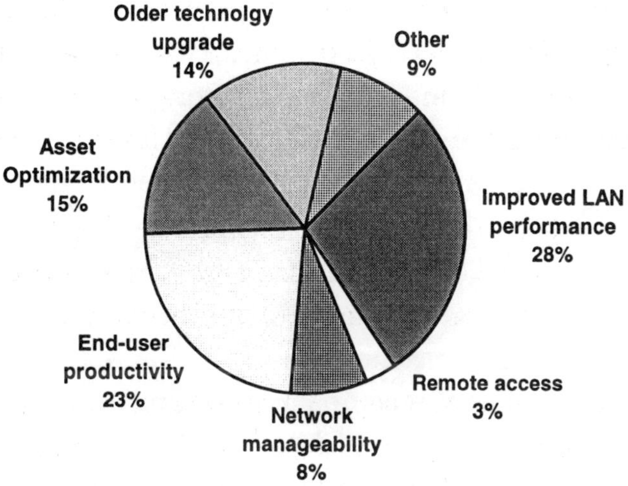

Source: IDC

As a business-critical application delivery vehicle, the premium class of desktop system is distinguished from garden variety PCs by its real multitasking operating systems, high-powered hardware, and extensive memory. Users require these capabilities to:

- *Maintain connections to multiple servers and legacy systems:* As companies build their network computing environments, the typical corporate PC will extend to file, license, application, and legacy servers. Preemptive multitasking will be needed to allow these clients to establish several simultaneous communication sessions. With today's PCs, the 16-bit DOS underpinnings of Windows prevent systems from reliably managing live links to mainframes, servers, and other systems.

- *Provide reliable performance:* Business applications demand guaranteed uptime. Intel's 286 and 386 hardware lacks the on-chip cache and numeric co-processors necessary to run Windows, productivity software, and corporate applications with reasonable response times.

- *Keep intertwined applications running:* Second generation Windows products will use OLE to integrate spreadsheets, graphics, and query tools in compound documents. C/S systems will also build links between desktop tools and corporate applications.

- *Enhance high-end graphics:* Graphics, CD-ROM drives, and other hardware features are items that were formerly considered add-ons. They now have become standard features, and corporate PCs will be able to run a much richer set of applications because of them.

New corporate PCs will, by definition, be nodes on networks. This characteristic will require a higher level of hardware integration than has been necessary on the productivity desktop. For example, LAN adapters, "systems-management-smart" components, and high-powered graphics adapters have become an assumed part of the basic PC package. As multimedia interfaces appear in applications, CD-ROM drives have become a fixture.

In this new environment, large system vendors who have long histories with more complex systems and applications will recapture some of their advantages of the past. Conversely, it will be harder for "overnight wonders" to sell commodity systems on the basis of price alone. This competition has produced tensions among PC vendors, especially in terms of distribution channels.

The return of competition to the OS market and the appearance of a new set of corporate PC application needs will motivate the software world. Desktop Independent Software Vendors (ISVs) must expand their view of PC software. As C/S grows, users will want new types of packaged applications and tools for their desktop PCs. Corporate PCs will need SQL query tools and communications products such as Lotus Notes and Rumba.

New software bundling opportunities will appear. C/S applications vendors such as PeopleSoft, Park City Group, and SQL Financials will be popular partnering prospects for desktop interactive televisions (ITVs) and corporate PC hardware makers. Shrink-wrapping client-side portions of new third-party business applications will help accounts move more easily to the new paradigm.

The emergence of the corporate PC will reorient distribution away from the low-end direct mail bias of the past few years. In fact, traditional PC value-added resellers (VARs) will experience a wave of growth as the focus of the market shifts back to corporate desktops. A complex corporate PC world brings two new opportunities for outsourcers:

1. *Corporate PC support packages*: As hefty PCs become an integral part of corporate computing, large companies will insist on "cradle-to-grave" hardware support options. "Early outsourcers" will be able to make a compelling case: "Hire us to write C/S applications, then rely on us as a single-source supplier for installation and maintenance of your enterprise network."

2. *"Corporate PC help desks:"* The help desk scope expands as users wade through graphical environments and contend with linked desktop tools alongside corporate applications. Accessing data and learning how to use it in conjunction with several tools and applications will become a typical source of problems. Outsourcers who can deliver online answers to these new questions will find a ready market.

Types of PC configurations bought by the corporate customers can be summarized as:

- *Business PCs*: Systems focused on C/S applications. These devices have higher power configurations and more advanced features. Built-in networking, communications software, and query tools will be essential. Customers will look to early outsourcers for service and support.

- *General PCs*: These products will soon become personal productivity "appliances," coming out of the box with bundled suites of productivity applications and mail front-ends. Accounts can continue to look to their current channels as a source of supply.

- *Mobile devices*: For now, accounts can view their notebook PCs in a similar vein as their general desktops. After all, most notebooks are just productivity desktops with reduced functionality. However, as mobile C/S applications are built, companies will need to review their platform choices, configurations, and support model.

Terminals now focus on the graphics and multimedia niches of the market. For instance, DEC has unveiled a network terminal that uses Microsoft's Windows 3.1 as its local windows manager to enable users to multitask between eight live host sessions. The VT LAN40, preconfigured for use with Ethernet networks, includes built-in support for TCP/IP, DECnet, and Local Area Transport (LAT) network protocols. According to DEC officials in Maynard, Massachusetts the Windows 3.1, network protocols, and emulation programming are burned into local read-only memory (ROM) to incorporate this level of local functionality.

Chapter 4

Software Development and Maintenance

Why Software Is the Key to Interoperability

The IT management who have their hardware and networking infrastructure in place must face the toughest challenge yet: Implementing applications. Interoperability is an important consideration, and so is integration. Applications must be able to work together, and must comply with whatever protocols are being used. On today's networks, end-to-end connectivity is necessary. With today's C/S systems, compatibility is necessary. Managers are typically looking for ways to integrate incompatible messaging systems and connect them to the Internet, and integrate heterogeneous systems in a way that appears seamless to the user. To date, there is no universal interface for both systems and networks. Middleware, the glue that separates applications from the underlying operating systems and network infrastructure, has become an important technology for connectivity.

Application software is the value-added component of the future for IT organizations. As hardware becomes more standardized – desktop interfaces become more graphically customizable at the user level and the Internet assists in the network infrastructure – the real challenge in integration is the software, in terms of both applications and tools.

Vendors and users realize the value of the application software that runs in the enterprise today. Migration tools and strategies are the basics of systems integration vendors because they know how much value the application software adds to the business operations. As an IT manager, one should be aware of the commercial value the internal applications – both custom and off-the-shelf – bring to the business operations, and how hard they would be to replace. When considering future strategies with the current urge to migrate/downsize, remember the efforts and costs the application software carries. The current issues of standard application interfaces, database management, object-oriented development, and the maintenance and support of software all factor into the value of the application software environment already installed in the organization. Remember, software is the key to interoperability because it connects the systems and networks like no hub, cable or router can.

Approaches to Cross-Platform Development

Cross-platform applications are more difficult to develop than single platform applications, and often run less optimally despite today's cross-platform application development tools. Cross-platform applications may last longer, however, which justifies their resource costs. The same front-end running with a variety of GUIs cannot exploit the advantages of individual operating systems as fully as platform-dedicated applications, at least not without substantial code additions. When buying cross-platform development tools, the best and tightest solution may be the one that works specifically with those platforms for which they are developed. Examples of cross-platform tools currently on the market include Uniface, JY-ACC's JAM, Neuron Data's C/S Elements, Blyth's Omnis 7, Oracle's Developer 2000, and PowerBuilder.

Many legacy applications haphazardly pieced together for a single platform are still here 20 years later. As a result, the "disposable application" argument is no longer valid because code written today may eventually be used on platforms that have yet to be invented, by users who have not yet been born. Given the possibility of that heady scenario, and given that fourth generation language (4GL) cross-platform tools are rapidly moving into the development mainstream, creating platform-independent applications is a very important issue to consider.

Another driving force for platform-independent applications is Web server usage, which promotes the deployment of mixed OS environments. The use of Java and HTML application environments has accelerated the interest in heterogeneous system development. Developers welcome cross-platform tools because they increase the market size for any single application.

The downside of cross-platform development is the trade-off of optimization gained by using single target platforms. Higher performance might be achieved with a single systems environment through the exploitation of more OS features going directly to the platform. With increasing maturity and technical improvements in compiler and interpreter design, the performance difference between using a high-level, cross-platform tool and one built with a more demanding, less flexible tool can be negligible.

Will a cross-platform approach work for any company? The answer is not only based on technical and logistical issues, but organization philosophy. For cross-platform development to succeed, there must be a sound organizational philosophy and valid business activity. Platform specificity poses a threat to the long-term economic payoff from development efforts. The efforts must be aided by the best development tools available for the job, which in itself is a major challenge for tool selection.

The main criteria to consider when evaluating cross-platform application development tools include the depth and breadth of GUI and database support, and the tool's ability to adhere to GUI standards. Verify how easily one can make changes to applications that live on multiple platforms and how they can split processing on the client and on the server. The easiest possible way to check this information may be to go to a user group meeting for that tool vendor's products. Talk to other users about their experiences to gain an accurate impression of the product's difficulty level.

OLE and OpenDoc

OLE automation provides a common application infrastructure enabling C/S developers to easily bind several applications together. This binding lets each application use the services of the others, but the advantages of using OLE automation go further. Remote OLE automation can now reach across networks, allowing developers to create multitiered C/S applications using OLE as the plumbing and wiring. Although OLE has been in Microsoft applications and operating systems for years, OLE automation has been impractical for C/S developers until the recent development of certain OLE automation tools.

As Microsoft's distributed OLE approaches with even more distributed object capabilities, remote OLE automation could be the best way to build three-tier

C/S applications because there is no commitment to proprietary technology, that is if Microsoft standards are not considered proprietary.

OLE automation enables applications to take advantage of other OLE-enabled application services. For instance, Microsoft Access can be used as a report server from Visual Basic and Excel can be used to analyze the results of a database query from Delphi. The standard interface is the key to successful OLE automation. OLE is meant to provide a standard object interface application vendors can use to expose any application-specific functions useable by other applications. An application that supports OLE automation should notify applications know of what it can do for them and provide an interface access to these capabilities.

There are two parts to OLE automation: The OLE automation controller and the OLE automation server. The OLE automation controller is the client side of OLE automation and actually invokes the services of an OLE automation server using the common OLE object interface. On the other hand, OLE automation servers have exposed functions or methods available for use by the OLE automation controller. For example, Microsoft Access (functioning as an OLE automation controller) can invoke Microsoft Excel (acting as an OLE automation server) to analyze and chart data from an Access application. Excel, as with other OLE-enabled applications (such as most of the Microsoft office automation and development products) can act as both a server and a controller.

There are two types of OLE automation servers: In-process and out-of-process. In-process servers are usually .dll files and execute in the same memory and process space as their clients. Out-of-process servers (sometimes called local servers) execute in a separate memory and process space from their clients. Out-of-process servers are usually .exe files and communicate with the OLE automation controllers using Microsoft's lightweight remote procedure call (LRPC) mechanism. Using the LRPC mechanism, OLE automation controllers can even invoke the services of an OLE automation server over a network. The process is similar to invoking a process on an application server using a standard RPC. The application makes a local call that executes on a remote server. As with most C/S RPC models, the client application must establish a session on that server using a user identification (ID) and password. This process is actually another type of out-of-process OLE automation server known as a remote OLE automation server.

OLE automation servers implement a specific interface known as IDispatch. IDispatch is an OLE interface that can assist programmers in implementing automation. IDispatch provides the mechanism by which an object can expose its capabilities such as incoming and outgoing methods. These functions are known as "dispinterfaces," which is short for dispatch interfaces. To invoke a certain dispinterface, the client (OLE automation controller) calls a single function – IDispatch Invoke – and passes a dispatch identifier that points to a specific method or property on the OLE server. IDispatch contains four functions: GetIDsOfNames, GetTypeInfo, GetTypeInfoCount and Invoke. Programmers can facilitate automation by correctly implementing IDispatch's functions. One method to implement IDispatch is to write it from scratch, which allows programmers to develop a greater understanding of how automation works. Writing IDispatch from scratch, however, can take a long time and involves many complex stages. Another method to implement IDispatch is to use the CreateStdDispatch API function of OLE. Developing a type library is another way to implement the IDispatch interface. Type libraries are created with an object description language and contain descriptions of interfaces and common object model (COM) classes.

The dispatch identifiers are generated by OLE's Object Description Language (ODL). At run time, clients must discover which interfaces an automation server provides. Clients can obtain all of this information from Type Libraries or OLE's interface repositories. The ODL defines the interface an OLE object supports and commensurates with CORBA's Interface Definition Language (IDL).

Microsoft, after three years of aggressively courting ITVs, is close to finishing a series of specifications – known as Line of Business Objects – that allows end-users to glue disparate vertical market applications together with OLE. Rather than release OLE-based frameworks that address specific industries, Microsoft has defined vertical industry standards in OLE and offered them to ITVs.

Unfortunately OMG chose OpenDoc, a method of assembling software components into applications, as its preferred way of linking desktop applications with enterprise object middleware. OpenDoc is being developed by Apple and IBM for the Macintosh OS, OS/2, and Windows operating systems. By choosing OpenDoc, OMG posed a challenge to some corporate IT shops because most have already chosen to standardize on Microsoft's OLE technology for their desktop applications. OMG's CORBA is supported by large organizations as the standard for object-oriented enterprise network development. OMG has been working on technology that will link OLE to CORBA-based networks but Microsoft has not been forthcoming with technical information for creating the specification.

If Microsoft had done a respectable job of implementing OLE on the Mac from the beginning, applications would be more interoperable, development tools could incorporate OLE Custom Controls (OCX) in cross-platform projects, and there would have been no need for OpenDoc. Microsoft is correct in saying OLE, under Windows today, delivers much of the promise of OpenDoc. It was only because Microsoft stumbled on the job for the Mac, however, that there was a need − and an opening − for Apple to define its own component standard and rally the anti-Microsoft forces. The unification of efforts by the OMG and OpenDoc communities is part of a larger battle for enterprise components control being waged between Microsoft and its competitors. Microsoft shipped an Alpha version of its Network OLE to developers in March 1996. Microsoft has also commissioned Software AG of North America, Inc. of Reston, Virginia to port OLE to IBM's mainframe multiple virtual storage (MVS) environment, and Mainsoft and Bristol to port OLE to various UNIX platforms.

Perhaps cross-platform shops will be better off in the long run with OpenDoc rather than OLE. Until there is clarification between the parties, however, C/S tools have been compromised in the short term.

The Fight for Object-Oriented Integration

Component software is poised to deliver on the promise of object-oriented programming (OOP) in the late 1990s. The component market was worth $100 million in 1995, but should exceed $1 billion by 2000. Components are prefabricated building blocks that hasten development time, reduce the chances of bugs, allow code reuse and increase product life span. Components offer many programmer advantages. They decrease development costs and increase the business functionality of custom software applications. Many of the productivity and reusability advantages associated with OOP are becoming possible with component software. Microsoft's OLE is believed by many to be the standard for component software in the Windows environment. OCX are now called ActiveX controls for Distributed COM.

In terms of object technology business benefits, companies will be unable to calculate the benefits of object-oriented technology until they first invest in object training, class libraries, infrastructure, and personnel. Generally, companies will not invest in new technology unless they can identify specific benefits that will result from the new systems. Some of object technology's capabilities are readily quantifiable such as the ability to easily upgrade systems, while increased time to market and other features are difficult to quantify. Experts suggest companies use a cost/benefit analysis to justify investing in objects because the technology affects so many concepts corporations value. Increased time to market, application reuse, and measurable levels of enhanced productivity will motivate some companies to invest while others will be dissuaded due to infrastructure requirements. Object technology is truly justifiable if companies consider long-term benefits.

According to John Slitz, vice president of object technology marketing at IBM, the evolution of object technology can be illustrated as: "Imagine a flock of geese waddling on the ground before they take flight. Generally, they are unorganized and unfocused. Some of these geese are sticking their heads in the mud, others are veering off in different directions, and still others are milling about aimlessly. The hope is that they will take on those beautiful 'V' patterns once they take flight," Slitz says. Users have the same problem with it, as shown in Figure 4.1.

Figure 4.1 What are You Doing with Object Technology?

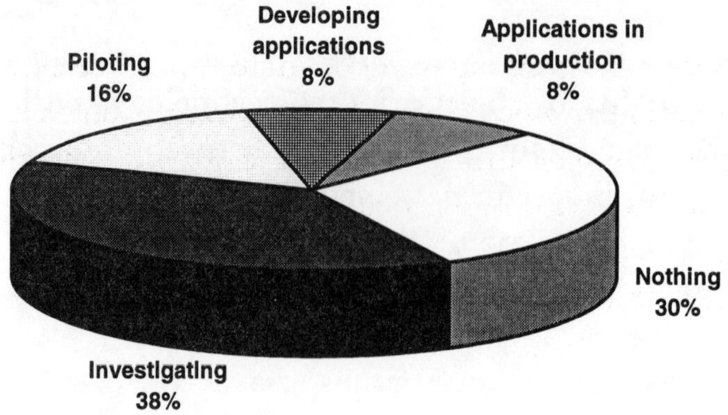

Source: Forrester Research, Inc.

For its part, IBM is positioning itself to be one of the leaders. In conjunction with Apple, the company was instrumental in creating OpenDoc, an architecture for compound documents. IBM's effort recently received endorsement from the OMG, which adopted a variation of OpenDoc as the first high-level application service designed for distribution through the nonprofit CORBA consortium.

Object technology was invented in the 1960s by two Norwegian professors attempting to create an easy way to manipulate a computer model of a fjord. Although it has been gaining ground, it has yet to fulfill its promise of seamless integration between platforms and programming languages.

In a field rife with paradigm-shift "wannabes," object technology is a truly revolutionary idea. Rather than rewriting code for each application, object technology proponents suggest every input should be representative of its real world counterpart. Everything from users to computers to blocks of code becomes an object.

Objects need a common interface to communicate. Standards such as CORBA and OpenDoc are integral to this part of communication. CORBA was introduced by the OMG in 1991 to simplify the interaction of disparate systems and applications. It is a packaging technique that gives objects a way of intercommunicating, says Anthony Brown, manager of object technology marketing at IBM.

CORBA provides a language-independent specification – the IDL – for defining interaction protocol through the application interfaces. CORBA can also help legacy systems interact with newer object-oriented code. According to the OMG, developers simply model the legacy component in an ORB-based solution using the same IDL they use for creating new objects, then write the "wrapper" code that translates between the standardized bus and legacy interfaces.

OpenDoc allows the creation of customized software using components from different applications and different platforms written in different programming languages. It allows large applications to be broken into smaller components. Programming with objects makes it easier to create distributed computing environments (DCE). DCE has been associated with another technology causing a true paradigm shift – the Internet and associated intranets.

The heterogeneous nature of Internet-based networks has made interaction and portability of software difficult at best. Proponents of object technology believe a standard interface such as CORBA could resolve many of these problems, allowing users to select systems appropriate to their work environments, rather than basing their decisions on compatibility.

Reigning over the creation of distributed computing environments appeals to many of the top computer companies. The promise of a market for tools that could grow to $10 billion by the end of the decade does not hurt either. For these and many other reasons, several competing standards have arisen, the existence of which threatens the very utopia that their proponents have envisioned. The object infrastructure will still appear, however, because of the cost-effectiveness of the concept and the ultimate business benefits it brings (see Figure 4.2).

Figure 4.2 Object Usage in the *Fortune* 1,000

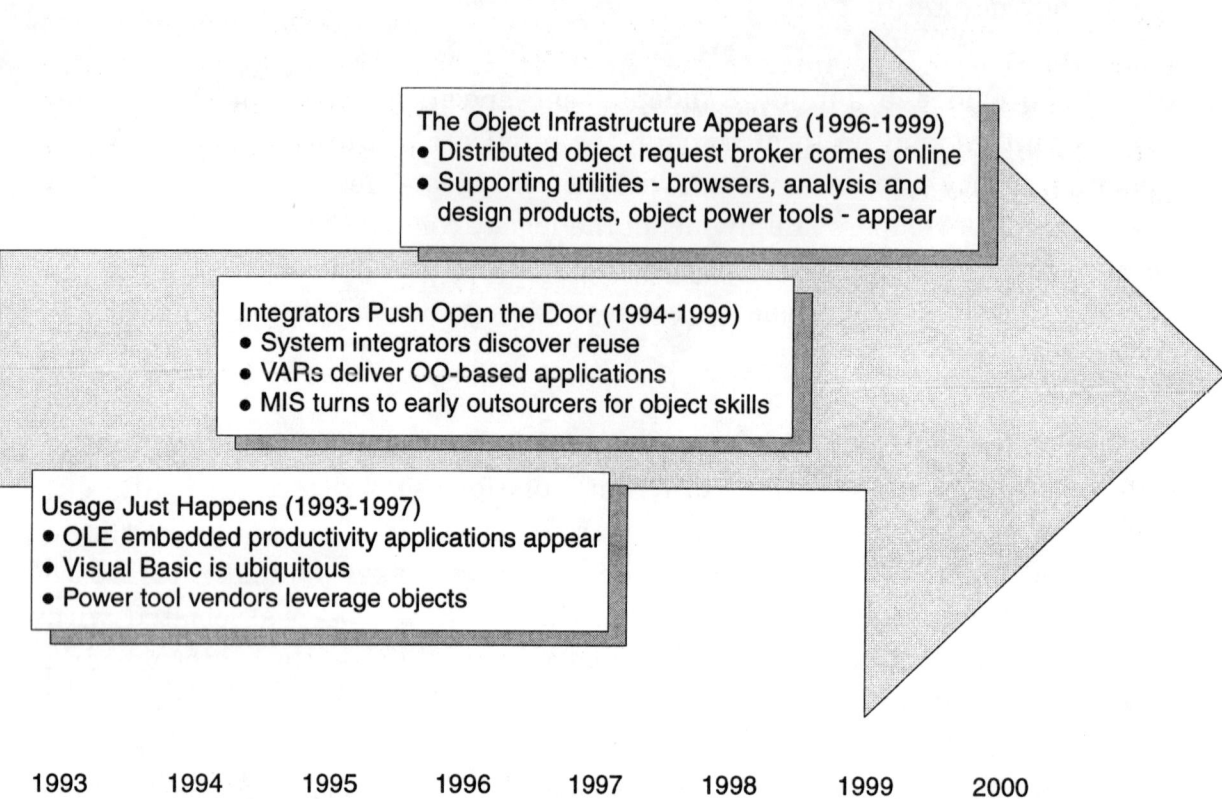

The Object Infrastructure Appears (1996-1999)
- Distributed object request broker comes online
- Supporting utilities - browsers, analysis and design products, object power tools - appear

Integrators Push Open the Door (1994-1999)
- System integrators discover reuse
- VARs deliver OO-based applications
- MIS turns to early outsourcers for object skills

Usage Just Happens (1993-1997)
- OLE embedded productivity applications appear
- Visual Basic is ubiquitous
- Power tool vendors leverage objects

| 1993 | 1994 | 1995 | 1996 | 1997 | 1998 | 1999 | 2000 |

Source: Forrester Research, Inc.

Microsoft has not accepted the OMG's vision. The company has proposed a parallel ORB based on its Network Object Linking and Embedding (OLE) protocol. Negotiations are currently under way to ensure compatibility with CORBA. "Everyone except Microsoft has lined up behind OMG," Slitz says, "Microsoft is trying to perpetuate its view of the monolithic desktop."

To include Windows users in the OpenDoc standard, IBM has pledged to port OpenDoc to Windows NT and Windows 95. Beta versions were shipped in June 1996 with general availability projected for the fourth quarter.

The question remains, why is IBM taking the initiative on OpenDoc, even to go so far as to develop a port for Microsoft? Several years ago IBM recognized the environment was going to require something such as OpenDoc. The speed of IT change requires rapid support structure modification. It is very cumbersome to change without standards.

Database Management: Across the Platforms

Relational database servers are the backbone of the global economy, but object database management systems (ODBMS) have provided an alternative for such markets as computer-aided design (CAD), documentation, and repositories. It remains difficult to connect clients to servers, but this issue is being addressed by:

- Microsoft's Open Database Connectivity (ODBC)

- IBM's Distributed Relational Database Architecture (DRDA)

- OSF's DCE

- OMG's CORBA

ODBC is a call-level interface for SQL programming and is a de facto industry standard; version 3.0 is a major upgrade that aligns it with ANSI/ISO standards. It supports Unicode, has better facilities for error handling, data description, and works better with large binary and text objects. An ODBC driver is a software component implementing calls to ODBC functions. The new version of ODBC modifies terminology to refer to options as "attributes" and has two new functions that return diagnostic information associated with a particular descriptor. Users have new ways to obtain information about columns and parameters and can view data as seen either by the application or by the driver. ODBC 3.0 also supports SQL3 locations. Microsoft's OLE DB uses ODBC to access data from relational sources.

JavaSoft and Intersolv have announced a bridge that combines ODBC and Java Database Connectivity (JDBC). The bridge promises to eliminate JDBC's shortcomings by expanding its ability to connect to corporate databases. The bridge should also make JDBC more competitive with the Common Gateway Interface (CGI) standard. It will be offered as a transparent part of the beta version of JDBC, which shipped on June 8, 1996. The bridge will initially support Solaris, Windows 95, and Windows NT. According to Intersolv, the bridge will enable Java to access approximately 35 database management systems and is a critical step toward widening the reach of enterprise data over the Internet.

IBM's DRDA, the company's proposed standard for providing interoperability among relational databases, has historically received little support other than interfaces to connect to it by the leading RDBMS vendors. DRDA was designed to facilitate users' migrations to C/S configurations, providing a standardized way to access data from IBM's mainframe DB2 database and other IBM systems, such as SQL/DS, on the Application System/400 (AS/400), DB2 on the OS/2, and RISC System/6000. Industry observers say the time when IBM can introduce a specification and expect it to be automatically accepted and supported has passed.

Developed by the OSF among others, DCE is an architecture and grouping of programs that ties disparate computer systems – including UNIX, Mac, PCs, mainframes, and mid-range systems – into a single C/S network. It is comprised of file systems, common security, and a RPC standard of integration. The major hindrance to DCE's widespread success is on the LAN and the desktop, where Microsoft and Novell lead. As more developers incorporate DCE into their products, distributed system development should become less of a problem.

The OMG established the COM-CORBA standard interface operability between OLE and object-oriented environments. COM-CORBA provides an internetworking standard for client interfaces in the communications exchange between mainframe objects and OLE-based desktop programs. The COM-CORBA client interface falsely appears as an OLE automation server to the desktop application. Prototypical examples of the interface standard have been tested, and software developers are eagerly attempting to integrate the new COM-CORBA specifications in products they are preparing for market.

The major trends in the relational database market are data warehousing, replication and scalability. There are also issues regarding the conflicting compatibility drives of object versus relational servers. Due to the difference in the structure of these differing database types, there is now a market for object-to-relational database mapping software to keep pace with the growing adoption of three-tier C/S applications. These tools simplify programming because it is not necessary to learn SQL commands or the inner-workings of the relational database.

The job of connecting clients to servers is still a complex task. There is hope on the horizon, however, due to development tools such as Forte's (Oakland, California) namesake product and Oracle's (Redwood Shores, California) Developer/2000, which not only enable programmers to create three-tiered applications, but can deploy partitions on multiple platforms. This requires middleware, such as DCE and CORBA, that can support distributed data access – as ODBC can – and distributed processing.

Until recently, relational database management systems (RDBMS) reached a bottleneck at the point where they received and responded to message traffic. Application developers were anxious to deploy programs that had hundreds – if not thousands – of users, and required a solution. Transaction processing (TP) monitors – standing between an application and a database and optimized for such traffic – provided a successful mechanism.

More recently, RDBMS vendors have begun suggesting these intermediaries are no longer necessary, but it is not likely large systems will be weaned from them anytime soon. Many corporations have deployed more than one brand of database, monitors will still be useful in balancing the load between them and handling transaction management across multiple servers. They can also be used to concentrate activity by bundling requests from multiple users and minimizing the number of license purchases required.

Introduced in 1984, Novell's Tuxedo was originally developed for internal use in AT&T's directory assistance and network switching applications. Transferred as part of the purchase of UNIX Systems Laboratory, Tuxedo has since become the leading open-systems TP monitor, claiming about 50% of the market and is in contract with more than 30 original equipment manufacturers (OEMs).

The main reasons for the system's success include strong performance, wide platform support, aggressive pricing, and outstanding tool support – for everything from Visual Basic on PCs to mainframe COBOL programs. As a sign of its performance, Tuxedo is used in many audited TP Council TPC-A benchmarks, citing the product as a price-performance leader.

The roots of the IBM's Customer Information Control System (CICS) extend back to the late 1960s. Consequently, many millions (or even billions) of those oft-referenced lines of COBOL legacy code are written around it.

Transarc of Pittsburgh developed the Encina monitor in the late 1980s and early 1990s before selling itself to IBM in late 1994. Encina was widely recognized as containing the most sophisticated open-systems transaction monitoring facilities.

When asked why IBM needed two UNIX TP monitors, Geoff Robinson, director of IBM's Hursley laboratories (Hursley, England) replied many customers wanted to move to that platform without sacrificing their investment in legacy code. This attitude spurred IBM to port CICS from its MVS origins to various forms of UNIX, AS/400, OS/2, and soon, Windows NT.

Database servers, especially the relational type, have become the backbone of the global economy. Every day, billions of transactions are posted against these databases in systems deployed in environments ranging from one-person contracting shops to multinational conglomerates. It is no exaggeration to say that, for example, the $1 trillion-per-day foreign exchange market would not be nearly as large without them.

Even so, not all users find that an RDBMS best serves their needs. Several vendors such as Ontos (Burlington, Massachusetts), Versant Object Technology (Menlo Park, California), and Poet Software (San Mateo, California) have released ODBMSs targeted toward situations that do not fit the short-lived transaction, row-and-column data format of the RDBMS world.

This group of vendors has found success in areas such as the CAD, documentation, and repository markets. In these arenas, the data model differs and an ODBMS can offer an order-of-magnitude improvement in performance and closer conformance to the object-oriented development methods and languages used to develop the applications that access them.

There are three major trends in the relational database world: Data warehousing, replication, and scalability. As corporate IT managers have begun to understand the specifics of using relational systems for transaction processing in the last few years, they have also started to build summary reporting tables to simplify line managers' reporting needs. Unfortunately, these managers also discovered they were destroying the performance of their transaction-based applications.

Data warehousing is the current answer to the performance problem: Build a separate database structured for reporting and analysis needs, and feed it frequently from the transaction database. The proliferation of PCs, departmental LANs, and power users has popularized a common strategy for locating the data closest to its users. This is the heart of the distributed database scheme, but it leaves open the question of how it all filters back to the corporate level.

Replication is the popular solution, which involves automating updates from site to site, usually in either a master-slave or a peer-to-peer configuration. In the first scenario, only the master can change the data; in the latter, changes are made on a first-come, first-served basis. Another critical consideration: Databases are simply getting larger. A 1994 *Business Week* article discussed data warehouse successes such as American Express and Burlington Coat Factory, where stored data exceeds a terabyte. Analyzing credit card trends requires an astounding amount of data.

Besides requiring ever-larger amounts of disk space, databases are demanding increasing performance from the processor or processors, as systems with four, eight, 16 or more are deployed. Some nCube and NCR Corp. (Dayton, Ohio) systems have hundreds of them. The database server must be able to use all of this capacity efficiently, however. Sybase System 10, for example, has had difficulty with more than four processors and has reportedly lost several customers because of it.

Many RDBMS customers have adopted object-oriented application development and find themselves struggling with the impedance mismatch between OOP and the procedural nature of relational databases. Object databases were initially hailed as the logical successor to relational servers, as they have gradually replaced network and hierarchical databases over the past dozen years. According to proponents, this development was only natural as OOP replaced structured development.

Market dominance never happened, however. Rather, problems with scalability and mission-critical feature support, such as availability 24-hours a day and seven-days per week in addition to online backup and restores, got in the way.

ODBMS vendors have been revamping marketing plans aimed at niches where their products provide unquestionable superiority. A number of relational database vendors are also adding or promising object capabilities for their products.

ODBMS has been most successful where application data models are the furthest from the row-and-column paradigm for which relational databases are best fitted. The CAD, document management, repository, and multimedia markets have been fruitful niches.

Another tack many vendors are taking is to provide an OLE interface to their databases, which should help overcome the current limitation that requires front-ends to be written in C, C++ or SmallTalk. OLE would also enable front-end applications to be created in environments such as Visual Basic, PowerBuilder, and Delphi. Given the cost of migrating, many customers will be content to wait for future developments before making such a major commitment.

Change is the only constant in life. Database hardware and software product development cycles were once measured in years; they are now measured in months. Business customers want everything faster, and they are more willing than ever to invest in technology, provided the business benefit can be defined. Database vendors are fighting to maintain this demanding pace, showing clients road maps of their development plans, and explaining how such business demands are being met. In managing this process, do not be fooled by the marketing "hype;" wait to see if the product actually delivers what it promises.

Middleware: The Glue Holds?

Although standard object technology shows promise for linking systems, vendor-fashioned middleware is often used today. Middleware is necessary, but what is it? Some people choose to call middleware the slash between client and server. In three-tier C/S computing, middleware is also the slash between server and server (see Figure 4.3). It is the software glue that allows machines to communicate and interoperate, typically using a well-defined API. Middleware insulates developers from low-level code by hiding the differences between platforms, operating systems, protocols, and underlying products. It provides the basic data transport from source to destination, giving users a single view into a heterogeneous environment.

Figure 4.3 Illustration of Three-tier Client/Server Computing

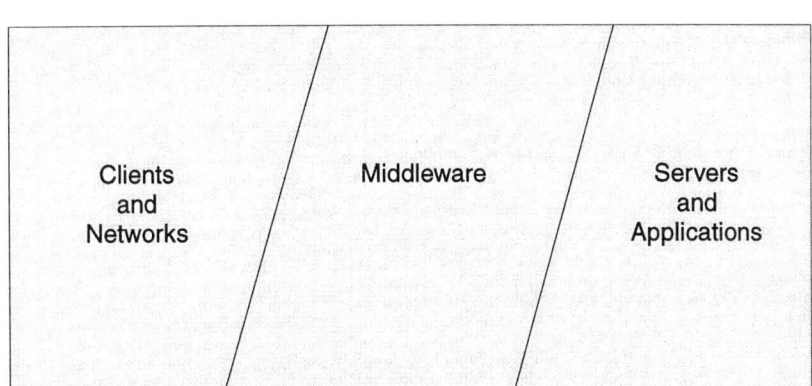

Surveys indicate 40% of America's top 100 companies now use some form of middleware. Over the next five years, middleware connectivity software will have a cumulative growth rate of 22%, predicts Input, Inc., a market research group in Mountain View, California. Input says middleware sales were $2 billion in 1994, and will reach $5.5 billion by 1999, which is quite an accomplishment for an area of software that few senior information services managers claim to truly understand.

Middleware responds to developers' needs to write increasingly complex applications in increasingly shorter time frames with diminishing resources. The middleware tools used for this purpose are interprocess or distributed function middleware that can be considered low-level, C/S "glue." They include ORBs, message-oriented middleware (MOM), TP monitors, and RPCs. Each of the services are generally independent of any other. However, some middleware products package several services into sets and frameworks.

Frameworks are packages of middleware services that may include non-middleware components tailored for a specific business function domain. TP monitors, electronic data interchange (EDI) frameworks for business

---

transaction management or management frameworks for system and network monitoring and management are all examples of middleware frameworks. Middleware sets allow several services to intercommunicate while providing a single API for the developer. For example, an integrated set such as DCE combines a RPC communication service with a directory and security service.

The problem in many corporations: Senior IT management has not really evaluated middleware and established a corporate wide standard. Strategic middleware, which by definition will affect the entire enterprise, requires input from key individuals throughout the organization. Without such feedback, companies may end up with a homogeneous solution that is not actually middleware for a distributed environment. The people evaluating middleware should form a cross-functional team, including the applications developers who will be using it, the network people who must support it with network bandwidth, and users.

For selection procedures, The Patricia Seybold Group consulting organization in the United States has produced what it calls a "road map" for selecting middleware to provide an optimal foundation for C/S applications. The map divides middleware into seven decision points:

1. Select a transport protocol, preferably a single one rather than a less-stable multiprotocol environment.

2. Select a pilot application representing the most important class of applications the organization will need in the next three to five years. This will let the company develop the requirements necessary to judge products.

3. Select an enabling service, which is the server-based code that supports clients with shared applications.

4. Select a category of middleware by determining its primary purpose, characteristics, and practical uses. Match the pilot application type with the network profile.

5. Select a middleware product.

6. Select application development tools such as ORBs, RPCs or MOM based on their support for required client and server platforms, overall

reliability, and performance. Also consider product scalability, openness, and cost.

7. Select middleware management tools to monitor, control, and administer the environment.

Distributed IS would be relatively easy to build if the required components snapped together as easy as building blocks and if the parts were as interchangeable as the components in a stereo system. The middleware industry is headed in that direction, but has not yet arrived because middleware management is weak and middleware interoperability is in its infancy. The technological checkpoints listed can provide some guidelines on what appears to be a path to new information and new correlation, as some organizations have developed new products because of the information revealed by connected pieces of data.

Common APIs: Allowing Users to Interchange Components

There are many driving forces pushing for interoperability at the component level of software development, including the Internet craze, the Windows versus Mac versus UNIX debates, and the ATM standards contingent. Sometimes it feels as though there are just about as many APIs as programmers. What policies and standards for APIs does a commercial organization hope to pursue these days?

- The Internet

- ATM/Networking

- Workflow Management

- Telephony/CTI

- Windows

The Internet

Webmasters can use APIs to provide interactive capabilities and work around difficulties associated with CGI scripting. A new generation of Web server APIs is bringing increased server functionality and interactivity flexibility.

APIs offer advantages because they require less memory for initializations and are able to "maintain state" so server applications can stay connected to clients without losing information. Moreover, because APIs work closely with servers' operations, more options for adding custom functions are available. Popular APIs include the Netscape API (NSAPI), the Microsoft Internet Server API (ISAPI), the Apache API, and O'Reilly & Associate's WebSite API (WSAPI). It is too early to tell which will be the longer-term answer, but a fair assumption would be either Netscape or Microsoft, based on industry demand for their products.

Netscape hopes its Internet Applications Framework will be the platform on which developers build a new generation of Internet and intranet applications. The framework consists of three main components: The network platform, the client APIs, and the server APIs.

The network platform includes the cross-platform languages, protocols, and standards for creating network-centric applications. The cornerstone of this is Sunsoft's Java programming language.

ATM

The ATM Forum ended its efforts in 1995 to develop a specific API for ATM, ceding the effort to industry bodies, including the Microsoft-led Winsock Forum. However, a decision has been recently reached to try again, and the ATM Forum discussed the matter at its April 1996 session and has again added it to their list of work priorities.

In the meantime, the Forum was expected to approve a semantic description to use with existing WinSock II and X/Open APIs, so existing applications can run over ATM. An OS-independent, Forum-specific ATM is a long-term goal because the Forum is contribution-driven and nobody has offered an API as of yet.

In December 1993, the API for ATM initiative began to give multimedia applications the full benefit of ATM features lost when users perform LAN emulation or run the IP across ATM backbones. Most APIs do not need to obey the underlying transport, whether it is X.25, Ethernet, TCP/IP or some other network type. Because ATM combines many traffic types, however, applications developers cannot ignore the underlying protocol.

Networking

Because Novell, Inc.'s NetWare is a popular networking application among AS/400 shops, connectivity and interoperability are major concerns in these increasingly heterogeneous environments.

To help resolve networking issues and influence the direction of NetWare related APIs, Novell announced the NetWare Connectivity Forum (NCF). The NCF consists of communications technology makers such as Bay Networks Inc. of Santa Clara, California; Cisco Systems, Inc. of San Jose, California; and U.S. Robotics of Skokie, Illinois.

The forum is chartered with defining a common set of platform-independent APIs allowing users to integrate an assortment of communications products and services with NetWare networks. The focus is on internetworking remote access, SNA connectivity, and network applications.

Novell hopes the NCF will expand the product choices available to customers while encouraging developers to build innovative NetWare solutions. The forum's first working groups will cover routing, WAN services, and communications management. According to Novell, other workgroups will be defined by customer and member input.

Workflow

The Workflow Management Coalition's Workflow API and Microsoft and Wang Laboratories' proposed Messaging API (MAPI) Workflow Framework have the potential to make workflow processing easy to implement on servers and desktops. The two standards will allow developers to embed workflow objects into E-mail messages and link back-end workflow engines to client programs. The standards facilitate data transfer between diverse workflow systems and allow workflow systems to serve mobile and connected users.

Delivered in November 1995, the Workflow API offers a standard link between server-based workflow engines and client-application applications. MAPI Workflow Framework is a combination of five message properties and two message classes that extend MAPI. Several vendors are embracing the standards, including Novell and Action Technologies.

Computer-Telephony Integration

Computer-telephony integration (CTI) applications start with the simplest automation of handling a telephone call to complex functions and operations such as voice mail, speech recognition, and text-to-speech conversion. The CTI API currently falls into two categories:

- *Telephone API (TAPI):* Developed by Microsoft and Intel to allow Windows applications to access voice services

- *Telephone service API (TSAPI):* Developed by Novell and AT&T to allow both PC to telephone equipment and Private Automatic Branch Exchange (PABX) to NetWare server connections

CTI applications should not be confused with voice/data integration because it normally involves the use of a PC for input and output. For example, a well-designed CTI system coordinates calls with caller databases so a customer service representative will have instant access to information at the same time they pick up the telephone.

Web-based CTI applications are encouraging the growth of LAN-based computer telephony. Network managers report their CTI vision is being expanded to include the Web, corporate intranets, and enterprisewide groupware. There are some limitations to CTI technology, however, such as the lack of standards and available bandwidth. LAN administrators are advised to change their view of CTI to see it as a bridge between two types of LAN technology and PBX technology, rather than as the absorption over time of PBX functionality into data servers.

Windows

Microsoft's attempts at fostering cross-platform interoperability and compatibility include Win32, an API for writing software that runs across any version of Windows; ODBC, a standard that lets applications access and gather information from SQL databases; MAPI, which fosters interoperability between multivendor E-mail systems; and OLE for sharing software code between applications. Microsoft has also embraced de facto communications standards such as TCP/IP and Novell's IPX/SPX protocol in response to market demands and to coexist with third-party operating systems.

Win32 is a set of APIs for writing 32-bit applications that run across Windows 95, NT Workstation, and NT Server. A subset of Win32 – known as Win32s – allows 32-bit applications to run on Windows 3.1.

The popularity of Windows 95 has initiated debate over the speed at which developers should be adapting the Win32 API used by Windows 95. Supporters of Win32 cite the standardization of Windows 95 and Windows NT in the corporate world as a vital reason for learning the environment, although industry studies show Windows 95 has had a slow entry into the corporate market. Others agree migration to the systems will be slow and developers would be wiser to focus on Internet, multimedia, and OOP environments. The Win32 API has been available since 1994, but is now eliciting new debates. Thirty two-bit applications are enticing to users because they are faster and effective for multitasking. The best advice for developers: Concentrate on learning broader and more transportable programming versus one particular operating environment.

API Practices

Forrester Research coined the term "corporate API" to express the theoretical application development model that advocates IT restructuring into two separate labor units. Under this model, central MIS would create long-term strategic foundations and set policy standards, whereas line-of-business IT would handle the building of applications that take advantage of current business opportunities. Corporate API is conceptualized to reduce development cycles and produce results more quickly. Several phases can be implemented to help migrate the IT structure to this model:

- The catalyst phase uses a personnel change in management or an unapproved IT organization audit to identify proactive IT leaders.

- Phase two demands the management team expresses its corporate vision.

- The transformation phase pinpoints any barriers to the strategy, which are then eliminated.

This approach moves away from the typical clannish or parental approaches to IT management. Figure 4.4 shows Forrester Research's ideas for organizing on this model.

Figure 4.4 Organizing for the Corporate API

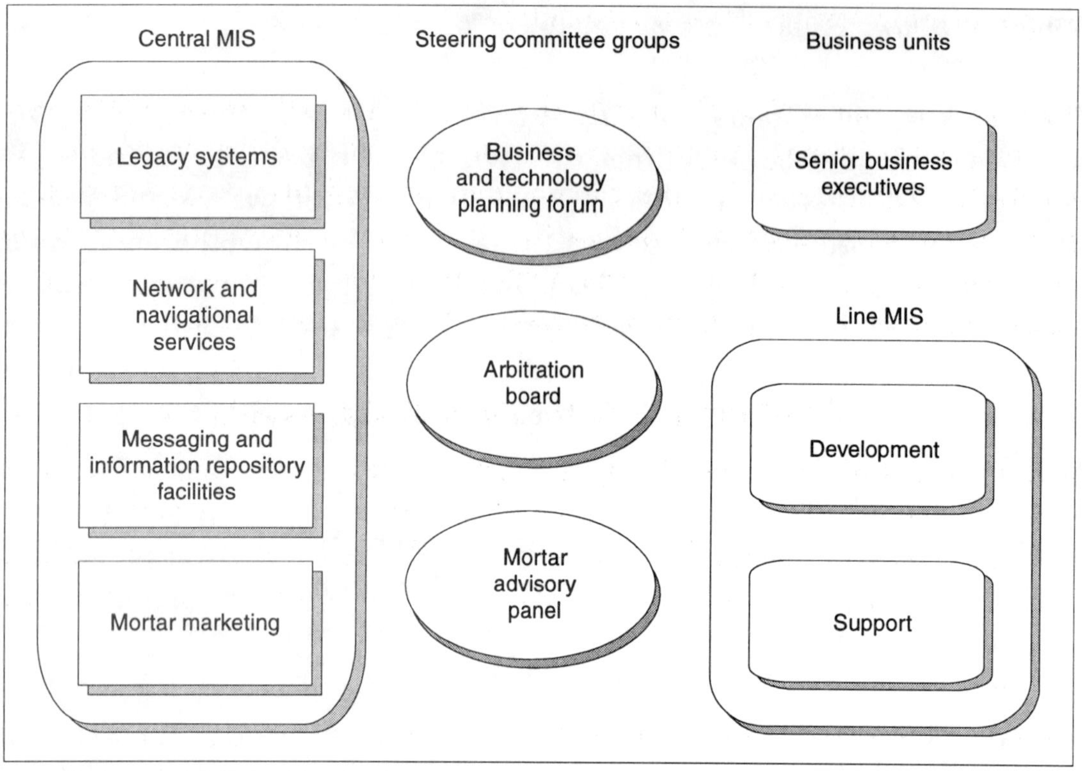

Central MIS
- Legacy systems
- Network and navigational services
- Messaging and information repository facilities
- Mortar marketing

Steering committee groups
- Business and technology planning forum
- Arbitration board
- Mortar advisory panel

Business units
- Senior business executives

Line MIS
- Development
- Support

Source: Forrester Research, Inc.

In this new application development model, in its purest theoretical interpretation, the focus of the corporate API is to accomplish tasks and facilitate the development cycle by sheltering business executives from the onslaught of acronyms that, in the past, have slowed the process. Here, the IT organization supporting the business units is responsible for developing all applications. This is the more efficient way to approach development – more efficient than outsourcing.

Another model is more market-focused in strategy with a concept of the "customer intimate," or the business unit and goal intimate. A Gartner Group study suggests 75% of all IT departments that do not retool to a market-focused corporate API structure by 1999 will be outsourced. Again, this is an example of the business focus that has made the IT department a key element in attaining a competitive advantage.

Yet, the changes dictated by the corporate API are equally daunting. It leaves business executives in charge to prioritize the development activities of the line-of-business IT group and central IT is then no longer in charge of much of the development coffers. In business, both money and information are powerful in terms of the office politics.

Regardless if one believes any of these scenarios will work, there is one truism: Development must be separate, yet aligned with the business objectives. Separation – and to some extent centralization – is necessary for efficient work practices, but unless the developers understand the business processes and the user needs, the application will be inappropriate for the business and will not provide the necessary business advantage.

Desktop Maintenance and Upgrading

Acquiring and distributing the appropriate software, the correct way and at the right price, is a major concern for organizations today. It is important to make the process efficient, flexible, and cost-effective. A recommendation is to efficiently use the network as a mechanism for upgrading on an enterprise or workgroup level.

A survey of about 2,000 European desktop computer users by the OTR Group reveals that companies are trapped in a largely unnecessary, expensive upgrade process and resent it. The problem: Upgrading operating systems, applications, and hardware are all interrelated. A new application, for example, may require more RAM, a larger hard disk, and/or a new processor. Similarly, a new PC or OS may require the newest versions of applications because of the lack of backward compatibility. Other problems include the need for training employees on new software or hardware (an average cost of about $4,000 per workstation for upgrades over five years) and the fact that only 10% of users need the new capabilities and only 20% of the new functions are ever used. Consequently, 75% of the companies said they gained no financial benefit from software upgrades. Why upgrade? If one decides to upgrade, how can it be done efficiently? One might consider the LAN at this point.

Despite the ever-increasing reliability and speed of networks and server software, many organizations still hold applications software on local hard disks rather than running them over the network. While this provides reliability in the event of a network or server failure, it is stressful and tedious for the technical staff, who spend hours reconfiguring software or performing upgrades by swapping floppy disks on a collection of independent PCs, a particularly frustrating job when they could be making use of the LAN.

If maintaining software via the LAN, the schedule for any installation can be made as flexible or as rigid as the network manager chooses. The user can stall scheduled installations within administrator-defined constraints or fit installations around their schedules, while guaranteeing the installations are made at or before a given time.

Installing Windows software is not just a matter of copying files; the Windows configuration files must be altered to reflect changes in the appearance of the desktop (some of the new items are members of program groups, for example, and many will have their own program group on the desktop). By maintaining software applications on the network, this simplifies the administrator's time and efforts.

Cost-effectively purchasing these upgrades has led to a new trend in software purchasing: The volume purchasing program. This need for the enterprise to be on the same release was one of the reasons why Microsoft developed its Select program. Select is a comprehensive volume software purchasing program that can reduce the enterprise's total cost of software ownership and help reduce the risk of piracy within the organization. Select consists of two licensing program options so one can choose the licensing program to meet the organization's needs. The program options are Microsoft Enterprise License and Microsoft Variable License. A company selects the number of licenses of the appropriate applications and receives a CD-ROM with the software on it to upload. The legitimacy issue is monitored several times during the year. By receiving a CD-ROM and upgrading across the enterprise network, the company saves time and money for applications upgrades. By running the applications on the network, it saves unnecessary additional licenses where they might not be needed.

Support Software: Help Desk and Customer Management

A Gartner Group report anticipates 90% of all help desk outsourcing contracts will supplement rather than replace internal help desk staff by 1998. Help desk staff can be insourced, temporarily outsourced as supplemental assistance with internal problems or strategically sourced using outsourced help only in special areas that need it.

Help desk software brings greater efficiency to help desk operations by providing network management, database access, work order request, and call management features to overworked staff members. Help desk application solutions can be modified to perform numerous tasks, including paging and technician alerts, that ordinarily begin to bog down help personnel. Indeed, solutions must be flexible, scalable, and capable of fine-tuning because personnel are always working on different problems. Users report help desk software allows them to group network problems into different that are immediately accessible categories. Help personnel occasionally neglect the software's ability to print reports, although these printed statements of problems and resolutions are valuable for analyzing productivity and network health.

Corporations are beginning to discover customer support or customer interaction software transforms the customer service operation into a valuable enterprise asset. Scopus Technology of Emeryville, California, Remedy Corp. of Mountainview, California, and many other companies market software that reduces the time customers spend on the telephone and automatically generates a database of the same customers' previous questions and complaints. Corporations are embracing the technology at a rapid rate; analysts predict the customer interaction market will surge from $400 million to $3 billion in annual revenues by the year 2000. The software is receiving an increase from booming intranet popularity because easily accessible corporate information can be applied to customer problems. Customer interaction software also can be used to support employees and other internal personnel.

What, then, is necessary to set-up an internal help desk or customer support operation? These suggestions may be of use (adapted from an original list composed by the U.S. Department of Defense [DOD], and the East Bay Municipal Utility District):

- *Insurance:* Secure management's support for a help desk/customer support operation. Get commitment for ongoing funding and staffing. Show them return on investment (ROI) figures, and inform management of the vital importance that the departments are to efficient operations and bottomline revenue.

- *Needs Analysis:* Determine the number of users and the products they use. In rough terms: A 1:200 ratio (support staff to clients) if the users are skilled, and 1:100 if they are beginners. For a customer support operation, purchase a suitable database. (Note: This is a critical step.)

- *A Few Good Recruits:* When hiring, look for a comprehensive background, including networking, hardware, and software. Look for strong telephone skills dealing with distraught people, and proof the individuals work well under stress. Also look for team players because coverage for other department members occasionally happens.

- *Lay Down the Law:* Implement department guidelines. Describe the kind of service provided, including time frames and guarantees. This may be necessary if the company is ISO 9000-compliant.

- *Problem Logging:* Let users know what services are provided and how to get help. Instruct them in what to do before they make a call (write down error messages, list the software loaded, etc.). Develop ways to provide a receipt proving the problem has been logged.

- *Plug In:* Set-up the communication hardware. Look for efficient telephone and voice-mail systems. An efficient E-mail system will prove to be indispensable. Be aware of time differences in different locations/countries, both in external and internal client offices, and develop a way to service them with the resources available.

- *Go Online:* Purchase at least one computer for each member of the support staff. Configure these systems exactly as the users' systems are configured. For a customer support team, have access to a similar configuration if it is not on a PC.

- *Who, What, When:* Purchase tracking software that features call logging, text search, and reporting capabilities. Why reinvent the wheel if the problem has been solved?

The key to a successful help desk/customer support operation is the expertise of its staff. Prepare to invest in ongoing training for the support specialists because the entire organization relies on them. After all, the person who answers the telephone gives the first impression of the organization, no matter what their role is in the company.

Chapter 5

Connectivity and Communication

To compete effectively, organizations are reengineering their businesses and using networks – among other technologies – to enhance productivity. Distributed network solutions offer the most dramatic computing performance for the price because they increase speed and flexibility and provide improved functionality to end-users. Achieving the optimal automation solution, however, is challenged by the complexity of the distributed network environment and the lack of trained resources to design, deploy, and support networks.

The challenges before the network manager are not limited to deciding which technology and equipment to implement. They must also determine how to implement the technology on a limited budget and balance internal political ramifications both from senior management and end-users. With communications and information more vital than ever in today's business environment, the need for a strong, secure, reliable – yet cost-efficient infrastructure – is increasingly important as organizations evolve and mobilize. The choice of equipment and service partners continues to be a major part of an organization's communications strategy, and the liberalization of the telecommunications sector is dramatically changing the role of partners.

Pinpointing and Managing Network Costs

Network managers are facing greater challenges in terms of connectivity, increased scrutiny, and smaller budgets. There are a number of factors that contribute to increasing cost and complexity. These hidden costs must be

---

understood to predict the cost of a network change. These factors include implementation of new protocols such as TCP/IP, IPX, and ATM, equipment such as stackable hubs and switches; maintaining relationships with multiple vendors; and new software platforms. Industry studies have shown implementing a new protocol can consume more than four-person months. These factors can contribute to the overall cost of network ownership – especially when considering personnel costs comprise up to 45% of the cost of network ownership.

Managing a network is never far removed from network outsouring. New management tools, additional personnel, redesigns, and upgrades can all improve an organization's productivity, but estimates and rules of thumb may not be enough to loosen corporate purse strings. In reality, network costs exceed the total cost of hardware, software, and help desk crew and network administrators' salaries. How one measures and manages the cost of the network money pit is the question.

The original motive for pinpointing total costs may be to reduce them – based on the "less is more" theory – in terms of the eyes of management. The main goal, however, should be to manage total costs for optimum results. Even if the budget is growing, it makes sense to target specific areas for heavier expenditures.

A manager must often pinpoint total costs either to defend them to upper management or find ways to reduce them. The necessary changes are often apparent but politically disturbing. If, for example, the IT organization's biggest line item is dedicated to wide-area telephone lines, but a FR system could be equally effective at one-third the cost, this changeover could be made before researching end-users' lack of training. If a costly support agreement for legacy systems costs more than converting the applications to a more flexible C/S system, choosing between the two options should be easy.

Structuring a cost model can be done by assessing critical input factors such as the number of protocols on that network, the number of estimated maximum users on the network in a given time frame, the existence of a standard desktop configuration, and the users' ability to change set-ups. This information can then be used to calculate a probability that costs will fall within a certain price range. Higher probabilities and narrower cost bands can be inferred with more inputs.

There are several aspects to a realistic cost model. Capital costs are the most manageable part of network costs and are usually open to competitive bidding. Support costs include vendor relationships, standards development, preventative maintenance, application help, and documentation. End-user operations are the largest cost area and the most difficult to numerically quantify because they are not always anticipated and can arise from inadequate support and lack of expertise. Also, disaster planning funds should be allocated when considering the potential cost of a disaster, as in a network crash or serious data loss. Backup operations should be regularly scheduled and regarded as a regularly financed cost item. Careful research can help an organization determine total costs; spending money to cut risks and recover from disasters is important.

When considering these cost issues, one must assess the risk adversity factor of the IT organization. The trade-off for reduced costs is increased risk vulnerability. For example, some administration, support, and operations costs can be reduced by loading users' applications from servers or providing users with diskless PCs. Without access to a server, however, these users are dumb terminals. When a server, device or network is essential to the organization's operations, a few hours of downtime can affect profit and cause the loss of the business.

There are several approaches to minimizing server and network downtime. In general, the goal is to spend resources on capital equipment, software or process improvements that cost less than the downtime their failure would produce. A backup power supply, for example, may be justified if one's system requires more than the orderly shutdown provided by an uninterruptible power system (UPS).

Many of the costs detailed are subtle and difficult to precisely quantify, but most can be gauged using known techniques that help identify the best method of controlling overall costs.

There also are intangible costs: How many customers will decide not to deal with the company again after playing "telephone tag" because a network was down? How much productivity will be lost from a demoralized employee who had to reconstruct a five-page memo wiped out by a network crash? Though their financial value may be impossible to calculate, these factors should be weighed in any decisions to enhance reliability and performance.

ATM Standards and Alternatives

There is general agreement that ATM is the wave of the future for communications. In some situations, ATM is the only technology capable of supporting an enterprise network's requirements. ATM can transport and switch all traffic types – voice, data, and video – from desktop to wide area and in carrier services including broadband to the home.

The private network market is split by the supplier offerings into desktop, building/campus, and wide area. Each vendor approaches these segments differently. However, the major differences among vendors are the markets they address and whether they have a solution that integrates voice and video.

ATM is being implemented in corporate networks for two main reasons:

Network congestion caused by growth in application traffic (this can be as simple as an increase in attached documents and graphics in an E-mail system).

New applications – often multimedia-based – need the performance of ATM to satisfy response time and bandwidth requirements.

Much of the business case for ATM revolves around network management issues: Doing more (higher bandwidth) with less (money); easier moves, adds, and change management; and improved usage monitoring and network policy management, all in a way that promotes scalability and migration and protects customers' invested dollars. This is shown in Figure 5.1, with a question posed by Forrester Research to 33 companies interested in ATM.

Figure 5.1 What Would Accelerate Your ATM Plans?

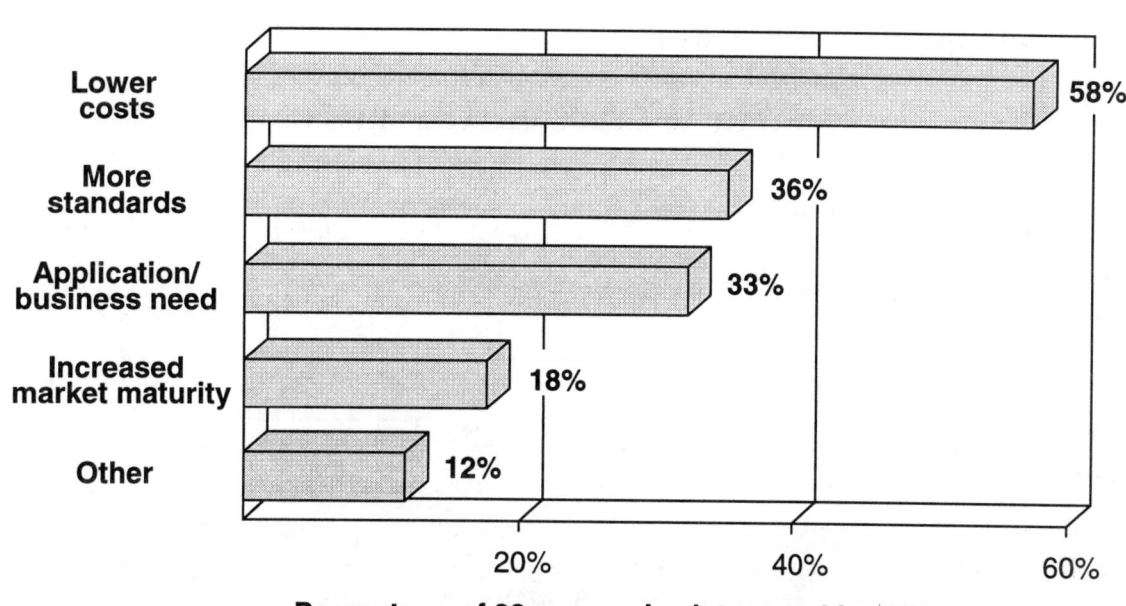

Percentage of 33 companies interested in ATM

Source: Forrester Research, Inc.

What about the emerging multimedia applications that have justified the increased bandwidth ATM delivers? Early adopters have successfully implemented ATM to support multimedia application. These applications tend to be in education, research, and engineering, where large amounts of data must be transmitted in a reasonable time. There are also implementations on Wall Street and other financial centers, where predictable response time is critical.

ATM switching is finding favor as the backbone of computer networks and WAN access services, but its support as a LAN technology appears to be fading. ATM still receives high marks on a theoretical basis, but its deployment is continually hindered as businesses finds ways to outdo ATM on the LAN. ATM is a hard sell to existing network owners, because it is expensive and cannot run existing network software without emulation. As a result, its future as a LAN technology is being delayed even further.

No specific technology provides an ideal solution. Each has its advantages and disadvantages, which network managers must balance with their own

LANs and WANs need to discover the right mixture for both current and future requirements. ATM is the most expensive technology. In fact, a $50,000 monthly service fee is not uncommon. While its method of transmitting data, voice, and video in small packets is critical for real-time, high-quality audio and video communication, most firms do not need these capabilities. At $20 to $40 a month, integrated services digital network (ISDN) can meet most firms' need to transmit voice and data simultaneously across their LANs outer networks much more cost-effectively, and is more reliable than using high-speed modems. Yet traditional FR service is still the best choice for bursty data-only transmissions.

What about FR, Fast Ethernet, and the other alternative technologies available today? Consider the standards issues and decide what direction the industry is headed.

In the ATM world, speed can be baffling. It seems the slower ATM runs, the sooner it will reach the desktop. The basis of this paradox lies in the development of a new ATM standard: ATM25. Although ATM25, which runs at 25 Mbps as opposed to ATM's speeds of up to 155 Mbps, provides less bandwidth than other standard forms of ATM, the 25 Mbps performance should still be sufficient for the majority of today's desktop needs.

The attractiveness of ATM25 in comparison to other ATM standards is simple. ATM25 network interface cards (NICs) and hubs are relatively inexpensive and ATM25 works with Category 3 unshielded twisted-pair (UTP), the same cabling already being used for telephones and 10BaseT networks. Standard ATM, on the other hand, may require the more expensive and less ubiquitous Category 5 UTP cabling.

Although ATM25 represents an affordable option for a companies wanting to adopt ATM, the relative infancy of ATM technology means several questions must still be answered. For example, interoperability is a gray area with ATM25. One of the primary objectives of the Desktop ATM25 Alliance – which, at the beginning of 1995, was comprised of 32 vendors including Apple, IBM, and Chipcom – is to develop standards for ATM25 interoperability.

The FR to ATM interworking standard provides a means to seamlessly integrate FR and ATM networks. Several Implementation Agreements (IAs) have been endorsed by the ATM Forum and the Frame Relay Forum that make combining FR and ATM networks possible. Two IAs have been developed specifically for current FR users: Network Interworking (FRF.5) and Service Interworking (FRF.8). Both solutions protect current investments in FR while providing a migration path to ATM.

Globally, FR is becoming the transmission technology of choice for WAN users because it is economical and efficient. Optimized for data traffic, FR's growth has been driven by LAN internetworking, SNA migration, remote access, and Internet connectivity. Multimedia and other high-bandwidth applications are more suited to ATM where a higher level of service is required. With FR-to-ATM interworking, users can deploy both FR and ATM as necessary to suit their particular enterprise networking needs.

Frame Relay-to-ATM Network Interworking Standard

Network interworking allows connection of two FR end nodes such as FR Access Devices (FRADs) or routers, which are attached to a FR network over an ATM backbone. FRADs have no knowledge of the ATM backbone because the network equipment – particularly ATM WAN switches – provide the interworking function. Multiple FR networks can be supported by an ATM backbone, providing users with a scalable, high-speed option that does not require changes to the customer premises equipment.

Frame Relay-to-ATM Service Interworking Standard

Service interworking connects a FR network to an ATM network, allowing FR devices to communicate with ATM devices. With service interworking, users can coexist with or migrate a portion of the existing FR network to ATM without requiring any special software in either end-user device. Service interworking allows bidirectional Permanent Virtual Connection (PVC) management and protocol conversion functions, providing a smooth, standards-based solution for both service providers and end-users.

Fast Ethernet as an Alternative

The 100-Mbps Ethernet market is emerging in the form of 100BaseT and 100VG-AnyLAN alternatives. There are several backbone technologies (including fiber distributed data interface [FDDI] and ATM) available to users that may offer advantages over 100BaseT, but 100BaseT will make an excellent high-speed replacement for 10BaseT as demand for speed increases. Many companies are finding they need more performance than that offered by 10BaseT Ethernet networks. These companies are turning to 100-Mbps Ethernet as a cost-effective alternative to the more expensive FDDI. Both 100BaseT and 100VG-AnyLAN have the same data rate and use UTP, Shielded Twisted-Pair (STP), finer cabling, and hub-based topologies. 100VG-AnyLAN supports both Ethernet and Token-Ring frame formats, uses the Media Access Control (MAC) protocol, and supports far greater distances between hubs than 100BaseT. Most major hub and switch vendors produce 100baseT products, but few major network hardware vendors offer 100VG-AnyLAN devices.

Any 100BaseT implementation should accommodate long-range network architectural goals. Several vendors have posed migration strategies that rely on integrated 10 Mbps and 100 Mbps shared-media and switched technologies as steps on the way to ATM. A benefit of these strategies: Users need not evolve their networks all the way to ATM; they can stop at any point along the way.

100 Mbps Ethernet should be considered as just one of many tools in the network manager's kit, one selectively applied where it can best solve specific network performance problems. Ultimately, a true switching technology, such as ATM, may be the most flexible, scalable foundation for most networks, with shared media technologies (10 Mbps and 100 Mbps Ethernet) playing supporting roles.

Why ATM?

Even if ATM is never implemented, Fast Ethernet products will almost always be used in conjunction with some type of switching. Any network design and product selection process should include a close examination of how migration to ATM might eventually be accomplished, and how the 100 Mbps products will be integrated with existing 10 Mbps Ethernet and Ethernet switching technology.

Although issues such as quality of service have discouraged ATM on backbones where matters of interoperability and congestion are critical, they should not discourage use of ATM in workgroups where a single vendor's ATM products can be used and the network can be designed to minimize or eliminate congestion. In addition, the workgroup is the safest place to experiment with ATM: Any problems will only affect that workgroup.

The question network managers must ask themselves: Why use ATM rather than an alternative technology? ATM is an emerging technology, but there are several reasons for network managers to investigate implementing ATM on the desktop: Higher bandwidth, future-proofing, and better support for data streams such as video and voice that need guaranteed bandwidth and are sensitive to small delays.

The driving force behind desktop ATM implementation today is higher bandwidth. It is being used for data only, not for its ability to handle various traffic types such as video and voice. To address the data market, ATM vendors are offering LAN emulation software that allows an ATM card to resemble a superfast Ethernet or Token-Ring NIC to network operating systems and applications. LAN emulation requires some workstation-based software, which may be integrated with the driver, and a LAN emulation server, which may run either on the ATM switch or on a separate PC.

However, less expensive and easier-to-implement technologies compete in more or less the same bandwidth range. Switched Ethernet, for example, provides 10 Mbps of dedicated bandwidth and does not require a new adapter at the workstation, as ATM25 does. Full-duplex switched Ethernet gives 20 Mbps performance. However, if a full-duplex data rate of 40 Mbps is needed, ATM25, which is inherently full-duplex, might be the least expensive technology that could reach that performance level.

ISDN Facilitators

Why Acquiring ISDN is a Team Effort

A less expensive, albeit slower, alternative to ATM is ISDN. After 18 years in the shadows, ISDN is still suffering something of an identity crisis, although recent endorsements from telephone companies and vendors have given it newfound credibility.

ISDN is most often offered in one or two 64 Kbps channels, providing reasonable throughput for voice and data. ISDN hardware costs about two-thirds of ATM, and service fees are minimal by comparison, at $20 to $40 per month.

The biggest drawback to ISDN remains its lack of widespread availability, despite market demand. ISDN uses bandwidth only when needed, while the ring network keeps bandwidth available at all times and charges for every minute of use.

Telecommuting, the Internet, and videoconferencing are increasing the demand for high-bandwidth, dial-up connections, but ISDN technologies may have missed the market. Early implementors of ISDN found the technology difficult to work with, despite its attractive capabilities. ISDN service providers failed in their marketing efforts and frequently overpriced their services. Variable usage charges made it difficult to accurately predict ISDN costs, and the charges were frequently more expensive than leased lines. Installation could take up to two months and users found it difficult to get their questions answered.

Newer high-bandwidth technologies, including FR and ATM, are relegating ISDN to a secondary technology used to provide access for remote workers, small office employees, and videoconferencing. According to analysts, ISDN's best use may be as a LAN outernetwork technology for remote access to a corporate network. In this application, ISDN would replace high-speed modems, which continue to have problems with reliability and performance. Analog transmission, analysts contend, has simply reached its potential. ISDN could also solve some of the physical problems of managing multiple high-speed modems. Rather than struggling to concentrate the modems into a single physical space, network administrators could aggregate multiple ISDN lines into a single T-1 line.

ISDN requires more of a team effort because ISDN's vast feature set and the residual proprietary nature of vendors' switches require the network designer to take a different approach from that used with conventional leased-line based networks. The first step is to gain a thorough understanding of the technical communications requirements involved, including those relating to teleservice features, capacities, and physical interfaces such as voice, data, and video. This may require additional assistance from colleagues more knowledgeable in certain areas, because it is important to have a clear sense of the communications tasks that have to be accomplished. Remote LAN access is not a communications task but rather a business solution.

The designer must select the ISDN equipment and services that support these requirements, having verified the ISDN service provider supports the desired features. The next steps are to order the service, obtain the circuit configuration from the provider, use that configuration information to configure the ISDN gear, and install the network. ISDN can provide a multitude of connection options, and the company will receive every available feature unless it clearly identifies what is to be achieved with the ISDN circuit. This is especially true because the costs for ISDN from service providers can range dramatically.

Therefore, the networking management must be very clear about ISDN usage. A very important use of ISDN involves the mobile workforce. The simultaneous need for fast LAN connections by home and branch-office users and LAN managers' search for a dial-in solution that can handle both analog and digital calls, seamlessly, is the major factor driving the ISDN market. As a result, network services are extended via ISDN to remote home users, satellite offices, and mobile users. ISDN has also encouraged the advance of new technologies such as videoconferencing and imaging. Regular telephone links and modems do not provide enough bandwidth or reliability for many real-time applications. ISDN can be a useful secondary network alternative, if used in a strategic way with longer term planning.

With the Web offering a more graphical representation of the Internet, file transfers are growing larger and becoming more time consuming. Users are becoming impatient with the slower analog methods of communication. ISDN allows users to access these applications at a much higher speed; more Internet service providers are adding ISDN capabilities for this reason.

Groupware

A definition of groupware that goes past "software that supports group work" usually focuses on a single aspect of group work and a key application that supports this type of work. For example, electronic messaging is an aspect of group work, and applications that support this function would be considered groupware. Most users' experience with groupware has been limited; perhaps use of one or several groupware applications, but no context in which to place them. Thus, E-mail and mail-enabled applications users are inclined to view groupware through the viewpoint of electronic messaging. Users of forms routing products are inclined to think of groupware as a function of workflow automation. Users of electronic conferencing systems or the Web are apt to consider shared access to information the root of groupware.

Most definitions of groupware tend to focus on singular technologies with a relatively narrow focus. Because groupware is at the convergence of what had previously been considered independent technologies (messaging, conferencing, workflow, etc.), there is much confusion about its definition and scope. Because groupware should help individuals work together in a qualitatively better way, it should represent an integration of these technologies.

Groupware is not a list of features and functionality, but a platform type reflecting this convergence. A groupware platform can be represented by the integration of three primary technologies:

1) An *object store* in which corporate knowledge can be housed and managed: Messages, documents, forms, memos, and reports

2) A *distribution and access model* that allows users to easily locate and disseminate information

3) An *application development framework* that leverages the native underlying services of the object store and distribution/access model

A *groupware infrastructure* considers the requirements of workgroup environments. Specifically, these include:

- *Integration with external resources:* The origination of workgroup information is often outside of the groupware environment (for example, desktop productivity tools and relational databases)

- *Platform independence:* While groupware applications often begin as departmental implementations, many result in enterprisewide usage. Platform independence is critical to ensuring wide-spread usage and investment protection.

- *Mobility:* A groupware infrastructure must be capable of supporting geographically dispersed sites, including home, laptop, and notebook computers

- *Inter-enterprise applications:* As businesses begin to rely on customers and trading partners as essential players in the automation of business processes, the ability to seamlessly extend the application – from the start or added later – is an important part of a groupware infrastructure

No business process application can fully anticipate every situation. No matter how many exceptions and special cases are considered, users will discover new needs as they explore an application's depths and as new business situations present themselves. Any system designed to create, manage, and leverage corporate knowledge is of enterprise scale, and therefore, must meet specific criteria. It must support:

- The full breadth of client, network, and server operating systems

- Mobile and remote workers

- Seamless inter-enterprise interactivity

An architecturally correct groupware system that supports the convergence of communication, collaboration, and coordination is doomed to failure on an enterprise scale if it does not also contend with the pragmatic realities of nomadic workers and inter-enterprise communication (see Figure 5.2).

Figure 5.2 Groupware Definition

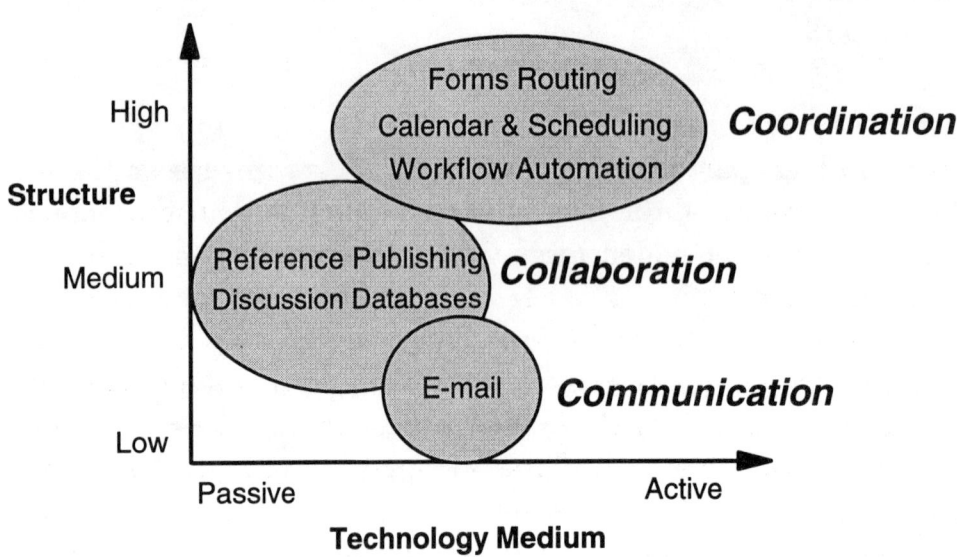

Source: IBM/Lotus Development Corp.

Figures reported by a British market research firm in its report, "Groupware: Market Strategies," indicated the groupware market is growing at a robust 15% per year, with the total groupware market estimated to be $5.5 billion by 1998. More importantly, 60% of that $5.5 billion figure will come from training and implementation services rather than software sales. This growth is due to the benefits derived from collaborative efforts and increased communication, both of which are enabled by groupware.

The fastest growing segments of the groupware market are E-mail and workflow, but even those segments are changing in this dynamic market. The report also states that one-third of the 1993 groupware market was workflow, with more than 130 vendors. This was still true in 1995. They also believe standalone E-mail systems, which today comprise 19% of the groupware market, will be only 10% of the market by 1998. E-mail functionality will be integrated into other technologies such as workflow, calendaring/scheduling or group decision support systems.

Organizational reengineering is fueling the groupware market because:

1. Groupware technologies provide many of the tools needed to develop reengineering strategies

2. Groupware is the primary tool used to implement reengineering programs

Business is on the verge of transformation with groupware as the enabling technology. By allowing employees to electronically share useful information, groupware cultivates and empowers the sort of team-oriented environment popular among management experts. With the help of groupware products, organizational hierarchies are likely to flatten, competitive cultures will become collaborative, and business processes will become more efficient and information-driven. Some of the wisest words on the topic were issued by Tom Austin, an analyst with the Gartner Group, Inc. in Stamford, Connecticut. In a spring 1995 research report, he wrote, "Organizations exploring the business applications of groupware technology concepts should keep technology and philosophy separate and ignore the latter."

The Web Role in Groupware

The Web has rapidly evolved into a significant network paradigm for intra- and inter-enterprise publishing and for other collaborative applications. Fundamentally, the Web is a set of protocols which operate over the Internet and over private, internal networks. These protocols serve as the basis for a C/S environment that supports information sharing and, more recently, TP and electronic commerce.

This rapid evolution has led many organizations to consider the Web as the basis for a much broader range of applications, many of which fall into the category of groupware and specifically in the domain of collaboration. Web technology has evolved from collaboration (dynamic information publishing) toward electronic commerce. While there will continue to be innovation in the collaborative Web aspects, it is likely the center of gravity will move more toward electronic commerce. Groupware – also starting from a collaborative base – will see its center of gravity move toward coordination applications. As the Internet frenzy continues, there is no telling how the groupware market will look in the future. The only sure thing: Groupware will no longer be synonymous with Lotus Notes because many companies such as HP and Microsoft have entered this market.

Messaging

Messaging and shared database technologies have become the foundation for workflow automation systems. Messaging moved into the workflow space by exposing its APIs to application development facilities and tools to create a workflow routing approach to automating processes. Shared databases have been similarly spread to support a tracking approach to workflow automation.

Electronic messaging is a form of transporting electronic objects among people and applications. The design point of electronic messaging is the asynchronous transmission of messages from one place to another. Messages can contain either simple or complex information, and can be delivered to specific individuals or groups. Messaging supports different-time, different-place information sharing by virtue of its store-and-forward or "push" model of transmitting or moving information. Information is "pushed" from the sender to the recipient.

Electronic messaging's transport system distinguishes it from other communication technologies. The transport is used to move or "push" an object from one point to another along a number of intermediate points (for instance, from post office to post office) until it is delivered to the ultimate recipient. Messaging provides asynchronous connectivity because the sender and receiver need not be synchronized in time. Therein lies the real advantage of this kind of store-and-forward processing.

Messaging is credited with revolutionizing one-to-many communication. Naturally, this quickly leads to many-to-many communication. As depicted by the point-to-point paths in the diagram below, the use of E-mail for many-to-many communication has increased E-mail volume exponentially. This transition in communication is not nearly as simple a move for store-and-forward messaging (see Figure 5.3).

Figure 5.3 Groupware Illustrated

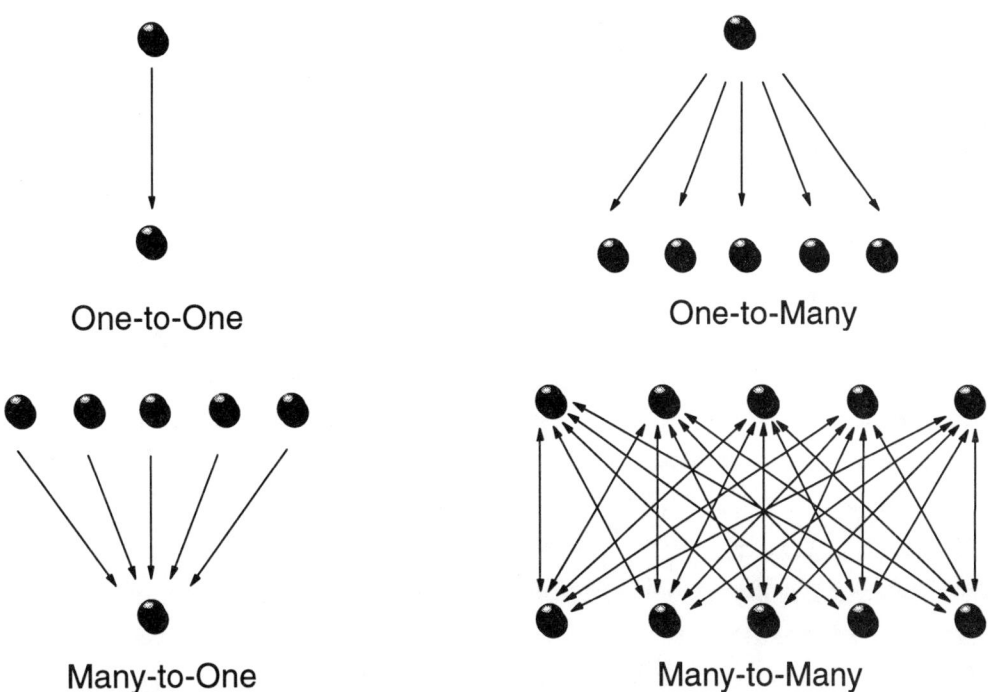

Source: IBM/Lotus

MAPI Standards versus Vendor-Independent Messaging and Common Mail Calls

Microsoft publicly discussed its plans for the MAPI Workflow Framework at the 1996 Business Process and Workflow Conference in Orlando, Florida. The new specification is an extension to MAPI and has been formally made available to the public. MAPI Workflow Framework is almost universally supported in the messaging industry, in contrast to the standards wars that surrounded the creation of MAPI itself. Users have noted the significance of a standard emerging for workflow, which has lacked a single guiding force, but they do not want to be dependent on a single vendor. The new Microsoft scheme will allow workflow software to interoperate with messaging systems such as Microsoft Exchange. Workflow management is a growing need because project information must increasingly be exchanged between more different users and departments.

Successful workflow application implementation requires the establishment of a common set of business processes. Workflow packages contain a middle layer that effectively routes documents to specific, predefined users. Although workflow appears to function in a straightforward manner, applying it to an actual organization's business processes can be problematic. Organizations must clearly define job responsibilities and individual security levels before information can be automatically routed via a workflow application. Before implementing workflow capabilities, managers must determine whether their enterprise software can accommodate a complete workflow solution and whether integrating workflow capabilities will complement or adversely affect other applications. Companies must analyze their commitment level to internal business processes and select a software package based on their particular workflow requirements.

During the last few years, three MAPIs have been competing to become the accepted standard for cross-platform network communications. Previously, developers incorporated interface elements from a third-party carrier such as MCI Mail into applications. The use of APIs allows messages to be handled at a lower level of the infrastructure. Microsoft Corp.'s Simple MAPI is incorporated into Microsoft Mail. The Vendor-Independent Messaging (VIM) consortium's API has been available as program development software package, and was utilized by Lotus Development Corp. in cc:Mail. Common Mail Calls (CMC) was an API proposed by the X.400 API Association.

LANs and WANs: Networking Integration

As the need for high-speed internetworking standards receives more attention, the deluge of new technologies becomes somewhat staggering. Fast Ethernet, FDDI, and FDDI-over-copper are competing for the LAN integration market; while FR, ATM, and switched multimegabit data service (SMDS) contend for high-speed WAN interconnection.

Through all these choices, a few observations become apparent: Vendors, users, and consultants agree the TCP/IP protocol has become more popular, bandwidth requirements are increasing by large increments, and some of the new technologies still have far to go. While high-speed WAN connections enable the latest and greatest applications – multimedia in particular – few organizations deploy multimedia on a large scale. While emerging technology holds vast promise, most users agree practical realities must hold true.

Therefore, throughput, cost, and reliability are key factors in choosing technology, and user concerns focus around stability, internetworking, and cost.

As the number of applications on the network expands dramatically, increased bandwidth has become a priority item. FR, ATM and SMDS have attracted such interest in the WAN market despite their respective shortcomings.

Routers also are important for interconnectivity because the use of routers in enterprise networks can be reduced, but never removed if the system is going to work properly. There are two basic approaches to connecting LANs: Direct connection through remote bridges or routers using leased lines; and connecting bridges or routers to backbone WANs based on frame or cell switches. Direct connection depends on the bridges or routers to provide networking functions. Connecting bridges or routers enables the WAN to carry a variety of data, voice or multimedia traffic. LAN interconnection is driving network upgrades. WANs are being developed through advancement of current networks, rather than replacement. X.25 and time division multiplexing (TDM) backbones networks are usually upgraded through software instead of being replaced by ATM cell switches.

Wireless LAN Interconnectivity

Another recent concern is the use of wireless LANs. The promise of wireless networking is persuading investors to spend millions of dollars in wireless solutions, but current technology has not yet realized the dreams of its developers. There are three types of wireless solutions, including wireless LANs, that enable users to wander around a building and continue using the LAN without physical cable connections. There are also wireless remote bridges that connect buildings within a range of 25 miles, and nationwide WANs that provide connections for mobile employees. These services will be of immense value to people who spend a great deal of time away from their desks. Cellular voice and paging communications have established a solid demand for such forms of communication, but growth in the wireless networking market has been slow. This lag is partly due to IT managers' concerns about integrating new technologies with their existing networks.

Although wireless has not reached once-predicted market levels, all technologies go through an unsteady introduction, lost between the over-the-horizon technologist vision and the need for management to keep sight of the bottomline.

As predicted by BIT Strategic Decision of Norwell, Massachusetts, several factors likely to allow wireless to achieve its potential within the corporate environment and grow at a compound annual rate of 64% until the year 2000 are currently converging.

The wireless industry is slowly moving toward standards that will both ease integration with existing networks and reduce management headaches. Costs also are declining. Finally, middleware quality is improving.

Standards are critical and the proposed IEEE 802.11 standard is almost through the long, committee-driven, standards setting processes, and is expected to be approved later this year. The 802.11 standard will play the same role for wireless that 802.3 does for Ethernet: It will define a standard to facilitate interoperability among products from multiple suppliers. The 802.11 standard incorporates an encryption feature to allay security concerns of IT managers.

The Mobile Management Task Force, spearheaded by Epilogue Technology Corp. and Xircom, has developed a family of mobile management information bases (MIBs) that extend the reach of SNMP-based network management software to incorporate mobile computer users. These proposed standards were submitted to both the Internet Engineering Task Force (IETF) and the DMTF for adoption.

Another standard involves wireless modems. The Portable Computer and Communications Association recently reached final agreement on providing a universal computer interface for wireless data modems. This interface is based on the Microsoft Network Driver Interface Specification used by most Windows-compatible, NICs, and will allow software developers to add wireless capability to Windows applications so they can work over any wireless data modem or network, including cellular, Ardis, cellular digital packet data (CDPD), RAM, and future personal communications service (PCS) networks.

Standards not only reduce the risk associated with new technologies, but they also ease integration with existing infrastructures. Several wireless manufacturers are now compatible with Ethernet topologies, while at least one matches Ethernet's 10-Mbps speed, thus eliminating the possibility of bottlenecks at the junction of wired and wireless networks.

Wireless has long held the promise of making access to corporate information regardless of location. However, IT managers concerned about bandwidth, standards and technologies, instead of solutions, were hesitant. Now that wireless has shown a demonstrable payback in vertical applications and with a host of worrisome issues on the brink of resolution, wireless is on the verge of becoming a strong complement to wired systems, in much the same way laptops have extended the capabilities of PCs and other corporate information systems.

Videoconferencing: Standards for PC-based Conferencing

Videoconferencing on LANs is set to become the norm, rather than the exception, due to declining costs and new standards. New interoperable videoconferencing products are on the way; videoconferencing nodes based on conventional LAN protocols are expected to increase dramatically by 2000. While telephone lines will continue to be used, videoconferencing will become increasingly dependent on LANs for the start and end of the connection, resulting in lower costs and greater flexibility. The trend is related to the move toward desktop videoconferencing, driven by declining prices and more powerful operating systems and computers. Audio-capture and video-capture hardware will become standard equipment on mainstream PC motherboards within a few years. The International Telecommunications Union's (ITU's) H.323 standard ensures compatibility between networked devices and existing LAN equipment. H.323 is an adaptation of the ITU's H.320. It is a suite of videoconferencing standards for switched digital circuits such as ISDN, which was ratified in 1990 and is now almost universally supported by videoconferencing vendors.

Desktop videoconferencing currently offers several advantages for personal communications, including the ability to initiate conferences as needed, share applications, improve productivity and lower costs. The technology is also useful in many vertical applications such as telemedicine. Desktop videoconferencing systems consist of linked workstations, each including a

---

microphone, video camera, software, and usually a video card. Video and audio input is digitized, synchronized, and compressed for transfer over most networks and telephone lines. Joint Photographic Experts Group (JPEG) and Moving Picture Experts Group (MPEG) are the common standards for compressing video. The regular telephone system without compression has also been used for videoconferencing with fast modems, LANs, and ISDN, though with a lower level of picture quality.

Videoconferencing will continue to use telephone lines. After all, the primary reason for implementing videoconferencing is communication between users at remote locations. Increasingly though, video conferences will use the LAN for the initial and final legs of the connection. The benefits will include lower costs and greater convenience, especially for multipoint conferences.

Global Telecommunications on a Regional Budget

Opportunities are emerging and the idea of local neighborhoods is no longer bound by geographic borders. Energized by IT, countries, companies, and institutions are creating their destinies based on local and global changes in markets, technology, and customer demands. According to some estimates, the global networking market is worth nearly $1 trillion. Many, if not most, global corporations today want one-stop shopping for everything from network design and deployment to network monitoring and management. Global companies want aggregated volume discounts. These services will enable these companies' IT groups to focus on developing strategic corporate applications instead of simply connecting users.

Today's global service needs include:

- Global, seamless basic and advanced voice, data, and image services

- Deep local support resources to care for the local customers' business operations

- Global reach, standards, and simplicity

- A consistent set of high-quality service definitions

- One point of contract and one bill in the currency of choice

- Local customization to meet the needs of a particular business

Affordable and ubiquitous access to IT is a spur to economic growth in every country of the world. At the same time, meeting the needs of multinationals for worldwide, seamless connectivity with deep local support is a major challenge that needs capable service providers. "We're still a million miles away from one-stop shopping," says Phil Barton, chairman of the European Virtual Private Networking User Association (EVUA), a group of 43 multinationals, each of which spends an average of $10 million annually on telecommunications. Barton, who is also network manager for Zeneca Ltd., a London consumer-goods manufacturer, says as a result, only about one-half of EVUA's members are ready to buy basic services from the carrier alliances.

At the Telecom '95 conference in Geneva, however, EVUA members demanded the carriers go beyond basic services to deploy a global multimedia networking platform based on ATM by 1998. Also at the conference, carriers and applications providers announced plans to provide higher-level, network-based applications such as Lotus Notes, Novell LAN connection services, and multimedia services.

Perhaps the rising ante is why even AT&T CEO Robert Allen acknowledges the era of one-stop shopping for global communications is just beginning. "We're only offering in the 5% to 10% range of what customers want," Allen says. "We're going to see it pick up fairly dramatically over the next few years, but it will take 10 years to really put it in place."

What does a multinational company do in the meantime? This leaves technology managers with the complicated job of internally handling all their companies' voice and data networking needs. It often means haggling with local telephone monopolies to install lines to connect locations. Technology managers complain they spend more time with regulatory red tape than fiberoptics; more effort trying to understand local customs than developing strategic applications.

The situation could become less complicated as the carriers focus on advanced, applications services. The carrier consortium includes:

- Concert, a joint venture of British Telecom (BT) and MCI Communications

- World Partners, led by AT&T

- Phoenix, a partnership formed by Sprint, France Telecom, and Deutsche Telekom

The Concert program appears to be the most advanced of the three main partnerships. Concert is a joint company created by a partnership between BT and MCI. The basic philosophy behind Concert is to offer customers the most advanced, effective telecommunications solutions from a single source. The company is a truly global business, with five customer support centers on four continents, offering multi-currency billing and 24-hour support in a wide range of languages. The support centers, like their network management centers, use common standards, systems, and procedures, no matter where in the world they are located.

The Concert Portfolio consists of four elements:

- Global Managed Data Services

- Global Virtual Network Services

- Global Application Services

- Global Customer Management Services

During the next 18 months, Concert will extend FR to 44 countries (twice as many as it reaches today); the number of cities covered will be increased to 160 from 53. Concert also plans to introduce an Internet gateway service. It will be offered at a fixed price, giving users of Concert's X.25 and FR services worldwide access to the Internet via BT's U.K. IP network.

This is just an example of the types of services and applications consortia offer, or are planning to offer, to create one-stop shopping for the telecommunications management.

To ensure the company's users receive all the network performance and services they need until the offerings become more constant, one must learn about regulations and tariffs. The IT management could negotiate an excellent deal for low-cost remote access cards only to see the savings disappear if LAN traffic has to be directed through 64 Kbps leased circuits or ISDN services in countries where tariffs remain incredibly high.

Countries with a competitive marketplace have more telecommunication services and lower tariffs, which in turn, determines what types of products can be purchased for LANs, LAN internetworking, WANs, and international private networks. A liberalized marketplace with low service tariffs also can influence the purchasing decisions of IT managers who must interconnect global sites.

Assembling a clear view of regulatory issues in each country is a difficult business. For example, some countries with basic service monopolies are allowing competition for services. Chile, for example, has one of the most liberalized telecommunications environments in the world and provides the advantages of full competition, including improved services and less expensive tariffs.

There are numerous global alliances of carriers. Still others are waiting for licenses to be issued. Until an appropriate solution occurs, the answer is to choose vendors with the best services that have the best chance of surviving over the long-term.

Chapter 6

Internet and Intranet Interoperability Issues

Managing Internet Usage

Corporate network managers are not in a hurry to use the Internet to replace private lines. Although, supporters suggest the Internet will ultimately replace private lines in the business environment. Nevertheless, the tremendous impact of the Internet and continuing developments make it difficult to ignore. Despite skepticism, arguments are based on the privatization of the Internet backbone, cost advantages, and standards-based security are convincing.

The Internet appears to have become a viable environment for corporate applications and has already significantly influenced enterprise networking. Demand will ultimately accelerate corporate Internet use. The Internet is also rapidly changing as pricing declines in response to the elimination of government subsidies and a shortage of IP addresses. Recent surveys suggest as many as 70% of corporate network managers have no plans to use the Internet as a replacement for private lines. Why is it so important? Why are people interested in the myriad of potential Internet applications when very few are in actual use today?

Less than a year ago, few were familiar with a company called Internetscape. The term "intranet" had yet to be coined, and hardly anyone suspected the vast and permanent impact the "network of networks" would be having on global business.

The Internet has had an enormous impact, and there is no end in sight. Corporate use has increased by an order of magnitude; intranets based on the HTML are redefining business communications, and electronic commerce has gone mainstream. These facts led to the conclusion that the other 30%, representing network managers who are seriously considering or already using the Internet in lieu of private lines, are onto something that may become an industry trend in future.

Although business use of the Internet has been more or less limited to non-critical, time-insensitive applications such as E-mail, Internet service providers (ISPs) and other Internet enthusiasts claim it will replace private-data communications networks for all but the most time-critical applications. Despite an appropriate dose of skepticism from many network managers and others, Internet advocates argue that privatization of the Internet backbone, standards-based security schemes, and the Internet's overwhelming cost advantages will inevitably convince corporate users to rethink their private-line strategies.

IT management must explore what has happened to make the Internet a viable environment for corporate applications, and what is planned to make it even more attractive to businesses. Almost every aspect of enterprise networking is going to be influenced: Increased demand for corporate Internet access will increase bandwidth requirements, corporate databases will be more easily and frequently accessed through the Web, multimedia traffic will grow, and additional database transactions security mechanisms will be necessary, thus creating another layer of network complexity that must be managed.

The Internet itself is experiencing profound changes. Because traffic has grown so rapidly, congestion is becoming a problem and IP addresses are in short supply. Meanwhile, heightened demand and the demise of government subsidies has ISPs rethinking their pricing structures.

When planning a successful Internet strategy, a company must carefully evaluate the purpose of maintaining a company Web site. The value of the Internet to corporate users is that it increases productivity and improves performance. However, the current usage of the Internet as a marketing tool can be a passing fad. The role of intranets is currently that of a process redesign and project management tool. The Web can be suited to internal use because Web software is inexpensive, easy-to-use, and easily integrated with other layers of information. Distinguishing significant developments in Web technology is simple for companies that have outlined clear business goals.

As for electronic commerce strategies – users, merchants, and financial institutions need a trustworthy system for ensuring that transactions are secure between the end-user and a company. Without secure encryption, the use of the Internet for electronic commerce will be hampered. Several vendors are offering approaches to solve this dilemma, but financial institutions such as American Express have been advising their customers about the limited number of truly secure offerings currently on the market.

The encryption technologies used are approaching a high level of integrity, but one problem is the U.S. government's view of the strategic importance of encryption algorithms. Internetscape browsers, for example, use an encryption technology deemed to be munitions-level security by the U.S. government's export controls.

One way around this problem is offered by Lotus Notes Version 4, which has a 64-bit encryption key, although a 40-bit key is the maximum that can be exported out of the United States. Lotus did this by allowing the U.S. government the means to decrypt those 24 bits. The U.S. government has the means to decrypt 50-odd bit encryptions – a capability no one else currently has.

With all the current challenges, the Internet represents a level playing field: Smaller companies can provide equivalent or better content than blue-chip organizations; the whole paradigm incorporates a large element of change, from existing methods of delivery to the new Internet-mediated model is difficult, and will be painful for many companies.

Business Purposes versus Browsing

Many corporations are discovering that providing Internet access for their employees also provides them with new ways to waste time. A growing number of companies are tapping into the Internet as a vital source of information. However, several companies fear Internet access may result in reduced productivity. The type of information being accessed by employees may also cause problems in the workplace. Two of the most popular U.S. Web sites are the Playboy home page and ESPN home page, a statistic that makes most executives nervous. Most companies are providing their employees full access to the Internet, but are also monitoring which sites are visited and for how long. Management experts advise showing employees some trust by giving them access to the Internet, but warning them their online activity and productivity might be monitored.

IT managers are debating the uncomfortable topic of Internet usage regulation because employee misconduct online can translate into legal entanglements for the company. An employee who violates the provisions of the U.S. Communications Decency Act (CDA) while using a company-sponsored Internet address may place his or her employer in jeopardy. The CDA makes transmission of indecent material over the Internet a federal crime. (This becomes an entirely different matter when global regulations are considered.)

Managers will find regulating employee behavior is relatively difficult, but are advised to seek legal counsel in establishing online employee regulations. The regulations should be summarized in a memo and distributed throughout the company. Managers should also investigate applications that restrict access to indecent online material. Add the issues of country controls (for example, recent announcements in China and Germany regarding Web material and controls), and usage regulation becomes an enormous issue for a company.

Does IT management know where its cybersurfers are located? Does the company try to guide employees' cyberaffairs? These questions risk starting arguments about privacy, employer rights, and the reemergence of "Big Brother" policies. They are, however, critical questions for senior management and IT staff.

With the Internet emerging as a popular meeting place with virtual town halls, shopping centers, coffeehouses, and pornography parlors, how does a business cope? Has the company established policies for the use of online services? Do colleagues understand their personal and professional liability if they post inappropriate messages?

It is easy for employees to get carried away in cyberspace because of the anonymity it appears to provide. An example: Harvey, a 54-year-old overweight staff professional, can easily be transformed into Brad, a 28-year-old bodybuilder. Everything is nameless and faceless on the cyber-frontier, right? Not always. Harvey may be easy to track down, particularly if his employer provides his Internet access. With an address such as harveyh@xyz.com, almost anyone can find Harvey's real name and details about his work and home. That is enough for a hungry lawyer with a client who feels she has been harmed by Harvey.

Harvey's employer can also become entangled. Imagine a chief executive officer's (CEO's) surprise if he or she picks up the newspaper and reads "XYZ Employee Nabbed in Cyberporn Sting."

The inclusion of the CDA amendment in the new telecommunications law adds to the danger by explicitly making transmission of some material illegal. Considering Harvey probably may not rich enough to be the sole target of a lawsuit, attorneys may try to involve Harvey's employer and access provider. What happens if it surfaces Harvey's boss knew Harvey was using his account for non-company business? The law says companies must knowingly transmit the material for it to be liable, but look for that clause and the CDA, to be challenged in the U.S. courts. It can get even more complicated when (in the near future) lawsuits start occurring across borders with plaintiffs in a different country.

A company can take steps to manage online behavior. Asking employees to behave is a start. Electronic monitoring can help some, but not much. It is easy to verify words against a lexicon of taboos. What about bit-mapped pictures? Monitoring patterns of bits may prove impossible with current security programs.

The first step is to check with the company legal staff, prepare a policy statement, and send an E-mail message to all employees. Follow-up with a memo on paper, a story in the company newsletter, and signs in the hallway. Encourage company employees to establish their own accounts rather than using the company's for personal use.

Look for emerging software tools such as Fresh Software Co.'s Time's Up!, which provides controls for parents to prevent children wasting time online or playing games. Fresh Software is designing an office equivalent.

Do not "pull the plug" on company-sponsored Internet access. Online information is too valuable a resource to restrict entirely; Internet resources can help employees make smarter and faster decisions.

Lawmakers and company executives need to understand the complex issues of managing online behavior. It is up to IT managers to start the communications campaign about online responsibility.

Moreover, this issue is attached to overall computer-related abuses which must be addressed by IT management policy. A study of 200 businesses by researchers at Michigan State University found employee use of company computer equipment for personal reasons, which could include Internet surfing, was one of the most common abuses. Tables 6.1 and 6.2 list a summary of the results of this study.

Table 6.1 Most Common Computer-related Abuses

Computer-related Abuses	Percentage
Credit card fraud	96.6%
Telecommunications fraud	96.6%
Employee use of computer equipment for personal reasons	96.0%
Unauthorized access to computer files for snooping	95.1%
Cellular telephone fraud	94.5%
Unlawful copying of copyrighted or licensed software	91.2%

Source: Michigan State University

Table 6.2 Computer-related Abuses
Most Dramatic Increases During the Last Five Years

Computer-related Abuse	Percentage
Theft or attempted theft of client or customer information	81%
Theft or attempted theft of trade secrets	77.6%
Theft or attempted theft of new product plans	81%
Theft or attempted theft of product descriptions	75.7%
Unauthorized computer access to confidential employee information	74.5%
Unauthorized computer access to confidential business information	74.4%
Theft or attempted theft of money	72.2%
Theft or attempted theft of product pricing data	71.8%

Source: Michigan State University

Uses of the Internet – Three Cs

From a professional business standpoint, there are three main uses of the Internet:

1. Commerce

2. Communication

3. Corporate Intelligence

Gathering information is a critical, frequently overlooked issue, both on competitors and on the market in general. It is truly amazing the amount of competitive information that can be found on the Internet. Examples are company distribution partners, new sales offices, press releases, biographies on key executives, and other key information not posted behind a firewall. For the corporate intelligence gatherer, the Internet is a wonderful gift because it saves time and effort.

This is also true for the journalist. According to independent surveys carried out in Europe by NEWSdesk International and the Columbia School of Journalism in New York, journalists' use of the Internet and online services

---

is dramatically increasing. (NEWSdesk is a high-tech online news network, available at no charge to accredited journalists and industry analysts.)

Both surveys signaled a profound change in the way journalists obtain their news and information, and underscores a clearly irreversible trend: Journalists are using online and Internet services for more sophisticated purposes and expanding their range of sources to download raw data and verify facts. The NEWSdesk survey was carried out with IT journalists and analysts over a period of three months. It indicated that more than 95% of these journalists find online services effective in sourcing news and information. The majority of journalists surveyed already had Web access and those who did not, will do so shortly.

IT management should, therefore, be well aware of the content of the company Web site and also be aware, through demographic services, who is accessing this information. The objective is to close any potential avenues for company secrets to be given away. These surveys show the importance of firewalls and other security implementations in the setup and maintenance of a company Web site.

Managing the Corporate Web Site

Many business Web pages are poorly designed because not enough forethought and planning was given. Corporate data is what drives Web development for many companies, and companies should carefully researching the Web's commercial potential.

Many company Web sites place the company's annual report online next to information about new services. Companies would never publish the annual report alongside a description of company services and give them to the same individual; there are specific audiences for specific types of information.

A company establishing a Web site should first determine its customers, what demographics segment they fall into, where they are geographically located, and what products and services they should promote.

Sun Microsystems estimates it can save several million dollars a month delivering support through a Web interface rather than through call centers:

The company knows those in its market segment are going to be heavy users of the Internet.

For other companies, a key component is their corporate data and the value they add through external transactions with customers and internal transactions with employees. This process requires more robust content development and management tools, including change controls, version management, and database integration.

If a company is contemplating a Web presence, the quality of the site is of paramount importance. First they must consider that the site's success is dependent on several factors: The quality of the content, the image that the content and graphics present, the brand recognition this site provokes, and the realization that it is not as easy to devise electronically as it is on paper.

To develop such Web sites, the market needs the kind of rapid application environment that exists on the desktop such as Borland's Delphi or the Expresso tools developed by Symantec. The industry has started to develop tools based on Java (a software language developed from Sun Microsystems), which has tremendous potential as a platform-independent application delivery environment.

These products – together with the wealth of new tools that add multimedia features to the basic Web interface – have the capability to make the CD-ROM obsolete as a multimedia delivery tool within the next five years.

Choosing an Internet Service Provider

The major step to getting online with the Internet is choosing an ISP, which is an important decision tantamount to selecting a strategic business partner. Automated Internet search engines can turn a Web host into a genuine production system. It is best to choose a provider large enough to make its future survival likely, but small enough to be sensitive to individual users.

Every day, thousands of companies urgently need to access the Internet for a multitude of business purposes. In most cases, they want to establish a presence on the Web. Finding an ISP is not as trivial as one might assume. Key points of discussion with a potential ISP include:

- Obtaining a bandwidth guarantee in writing rather than merely specify a circuit type such as T1

- Specifying, in the contract, a date the site will become "live"

- Seeking references from ISPs. Comparison shoppers can contact the services or turn directly to the Internet.

Paying a high per-kilohertz price rate does not necessarily mean one will end up with the best service. Likewise, paying the lowest price does not mean the worst service. Indeed, an IT professional should choose an ISP responsive to the company's needs and problems and have a healthy future.

Bandwidth is another issue. Selecting a circuit does not necessarily mean achieving full circuit throughput. If the ISP sells a company a T1 circuit (1.54 Mbps), the throughput should be guaranteed in the contract. Many providers will squeeze as much of their customers' combined bandwidth into their own, thereby lowering the average throughput for each. This is sufficient as long as the pipe size is known.

An ISP is going to be responsible for a production system that could be strategic to the company's success. ISPs are similar to service providers in other industries: Many will under estimate the amount of time needed to erect a Web site in order to get the contract. In the realm of Internet circuits, the most significant under estimation is generally is the date the company Web site will be activated. The activation date should be included in the contract and also placed on the purchase order. If possible, negotiate a penalty if the live date is not met.

Further, obtain and check the references of the possible ISP. Also check the Usenet news on the Internet, where questions can be posted about ISP candidates. Many respondents will offer their experiences including their successes and failures; while ISP advertisers will offering "great, reliable, and inexpensive" circuits. Choosing an ISP is not as straightforward as choosing other telecommunications services. Price/performance should not necessarily be the deciding factor.

Numerous ISPs have emerged on a global basis, but network managers are discovering many of them lack the resources to adequately support customers. Managers complain of unreliable connections, lack of service guarantees, and inconsistent support. ISPs cannot be blamed for all of the Internet's growing pains, but unsteady providers still frustrate network users because nearly all are expanding too rapidly.

Many observers expect a shakeout as already-fierce competition increases with traditional telecommunications firms offering their own services. The Internet is so fast-paced and the guarantees are so vague that managers often do not know what kind of service they will ultimately receive. Larger ISPs have their own major Internet intersections called Internetwork Access Points (IAPs); smaller providers must buy connectivity from these companies, resulting in slower connections due to more links to the network.

Managing the Corporate Web Site: How to Keep It Going

TCP/IP, the protocol suite on which Internet services are based, was once the domain of UNIX hackers and the large internetworks of colleges and universities. Today, due to the explosion of the Internet into the everyday computer world, TCP/IP functionality is almost a requirement for any desktop computer system.

Until recently, the software needed to link a desktop to TCP/IP networks had to be purchased separately and was extremely difficult to configure and operate. Today, software manufacturers are including TCP/IP software support in many operating systems, including Apple's System 7.5 and Microsoft's Windows 95. While TCP/IP software can be purchased to garner more or better features, the inclusion of TCP/IP software makes it possible for any PC to access Internet services, whether internal to the company, external or both.

Obtaining TCP/IP addresses and domains for a company was once an easy process. A company would submit forms to the InterNIC, the body responsible for assigning such information, and in a few weeks the company would be supplied with the requested addresses. As a result of the continuing commercialization of the Internet, the InterNIC now charges fees to set-up and maintain domain names and their associated TCP/IP addresses. These costs must be considered when a Webmaster is establishing Internet service for the company.

Normally, every machine on a network must have a unique IP number, for example: 132.107.101.138. There can be no duplicate addresses. If a company has already registered a domain name and has received its assigned range of IP numbers, then no further action is needed. If an internal Web server is a company's first venture into the TCP/IP world, the InterNIC's registration and maintenance fees (about $100 for the first year) will need to be paid.

There is one alternative to paying for a domain name address registration through the InterNIC. Instead, a company site can, instead, assign an arbitrary range of IP numbers to its system. This method works adequately if the company never intends to connect to the Internet, but if it does connect at some point, the arbitrary and most likely duplicate address will cause major damage to both its network and the networks of others. It is certainly a risky way to circumvent the InterNIC registration process, and it could eventually lead to much greater problems. The smartest and safest method is to simply make the investment of time and money to obtain legitimate addresses and IP numbers from the beginning.

Internetwork managers can have problems predicting network bandwidth requirements, and the dramatic increase in corporate Internet usage is making it even harder. Internetwork managers must deal with supporting Web applications and network bottlenecks created by Internet usage. They can solve bandwidth problems by implementing modular hardware, by segmenting employee Internet usage, and by building a flexible network with a variety of optional paths.

Another method to handle increased bandwidth usage is to utilize proxy servers. Proxy servers allow network managers to monitor Internet usage, enhance Internet security and improve network control. Bandwidth can also be controlled with the Resource Reservation Protocol (RSVP), a standard that allows network administrators to distribute bandwidth according to the priority of network tasks.

RSVP is an emerging standard designed to allocate bandwidth according to parameters set by the network administrator. These can include minimum bandwidth guarantees for selected traffic types and IP multicasting, which simultaneously sends data packets to multiple recipients, rather than duplicating the transmission for each client. For example, a mission-critical network application running over Novell's IPX/SPX can be configured to receive 30% of available bandwidth at all times with RSVP; a videoconferencing session on TCP/IP can be temporarily allotted 40% of capacity to ensure smooth reception, while other network applications can split the remaining 30%.

As corporate Internet usage skyrockets, network managers must decide whether their current bandwidth capacity can support burgeoning file transfers, E-mail messages, and the widespread multimedia applications on the Web. Top concerns include:

- How much access to give end-users

- How to avoid the bottlenecks created by Internet roaming

- How to determine the most cost-effective solution to a bandwidth limitation

From an administrative point of view, IT management must keep asking how much access is necessary to meet a business need. When one adds Java, animation, and sound, and then considers multimedia and Virtual Reality Modeling Language (VRML), the potential to clog up the system is there. Most corporate networks can handle Internet-based E-mail, and less frequent file transfers and Telnet sessions. Can these same networks cope with hundreds of users searching the Web for cool sites, playing intercontinental Doom with colleagues in Switzerland or researching competitors' Web pages to gain an edge? Probably not.

Companies must consider the ability to track the kinds of traffic generated so they can plan the infrastructure to support it. If a company is slowly rolling out Internet access and wants to provide unlimited access to a small number of managers, maximizing bandwidth could involve putting the group on their own network segment. The total bandwidth available is then shared among fewer people.

In the long run, modular hardware will play a critical role. The potential to grow router ports without buying a whole new router is one possible outcome. Routers can be stacked if the interface between them is as fast as the backplane of a larger router. Building a flexible network is the key. The link to the Internet might be a leased line today and something very different tomorrow so companies must consider how to build in as many optional paths as possible.

Another way to more efficiently harness bandwidth on the Internet is by using a so-called "proxy server." Rather than having individual client stations connect one at a time, which quickly consumes available bandwidth, requests for access onto the Internet are funneled through the proxy server. In the process, requests are prioritized and bundled together by type, thus maximizing bandwidth. Frequently accessed files such as certain Web pages, can be cached by the server, further reducing traffic and conserving bandwidth. Turning the proxy server into the central point through which all Internet traffic flows through the corporation also allows for a greater degree of administrative control and security.

Unlike a standard Web server – which is either used inside a company to distribute information to employees or to make information available to the public – the proxy server allows corporate users to access the Internet through the corporate firewall. Proxy servers require more proactive management on the part of the network administrator. They also offer another advantage: They let managers run software enabling them to monitor Internet usage to ensure it is for business and not frivolous purposes.

Security and the Internet

The Internet just may turn into one of the most powerful business tools of the turn of the century, but connecting an enterprise network to it without compromising a company's secrets often represents a sizable challenge for the network manager. Linking a corporate network to the Internet and retaining an adequate level of network security is a tough assignment. It is the job of the network manager to establish and maintain firewalls, securing their companies' resources.

At the same time, the network manager will want to make provisions for Internet users accessing information through a Web server and tapping into the outside world of available information. One method of preventing a network security breach includes isolating the Web server from the remainder of the corporate network, using a system that allows corporate information to be transferred to the Web server in realtime. Isolating the Web server from the rest of the corporate network tends to remove most of the security issues.

Procuring IP addresses for corporate Internet users is the first challenge IT managers face, which involves the installation of address translation gateways and domain name servers (DNS). DNSs provide an automatic translation of the address between domain name and IP address. For example, from DNS watt.seas.virginia.edu to IP address 128.144.3.098. This translation process enables users to continue using a familiar name even though the service's IP address may change. Address translation gateways maintain a pool of Internet addresses, and distributes them to end stations as they are needed.

Most organizations will need to set-up a DNS to register the resources in their networks. They also will have to set-up their internal DNSs that access the Internet and find external resources that people in the organization can access. Once an organization makes its resources available, security comes into the picture.

While security may be a pressing concern for upper management, network managers have other puzzles to solve. For example, companies contend with many different file formats generated by varying programs on several platforms, and these heterogeneous bits of information must be brought together. Managers are struggling to assemble the data for their own users; making it available to customers over the Internet only adds to the challenge.

The special requirements of Web servers prompted Computer Associates International, Inc. (CA) of Islandia, New York to introduce an extension to its CA-Unicenter systems management software tailored to Internet commerce. Called Internet Commerce Enabled (ICE), the extension notifies CA-Unicenter of events occurring in E-mail, file transfer protocol (FTP), and Web systems. These activities can be correlated with other events happening throughout the system so network managers can identify problems specific to the Web server. Also, network managers must carefully monitor outgoing network traffic to maintain bandwidth availability and acceptable levels of performance. Studies have shown once a company distributes Web browsers to its employees, network traffic increases for the next several weeks. Usage then steadies and may even drop a bit after two or three months, as users stop experimenting and settle into their browsing habits.

Whatever the usage, connections to the Web mean increased traffic over time, as the graphics and pictures associated with Web pages consume a company's bandwidth. According to Datapro Information Services Group, a consultancy in Delran, New Jersey, even something as innocuous as Usenet newsgroups can create traffic if users subscribe to too many of them.

Companies should also consider traveling users and those connecting to the Internet from their homes. These users frequently come into the company network through an ISP. In these cases, companies must be specific about which users will be allowed in, and cannot always filter out users based on the ISP because users might employ different providers at different times.

Another major challenge for IT management is the installation of Web browser software. While installing Web browsers throughout a network, managers must also ensure TCP/IP software is installed, and configure IP addresses if the clients have not previously used TCP/IP. For in-house users, HP, IBM, and other systems management vendors offer tools that will handle software distribution to PCs and keep it up-to-date. CA's ICE also has a client component that handles the software distribution and configuration of Web browser software. CA has set-up an alliance with Internetscape Communications Corp. in Mountain View, California to integrate the ICE client with Internetscape Navigator.

More management obstacles will likely emerge for IT as the Internet becomes an increasingly complex place to do business. If companies succeed in securely and methodically erecting firewalls, the benefits of using the Internet will certainly out-weigh the management challenges.

Firewalls

A firewall is a hardware and software gateway system and router that is installed in an enterprise to provide security in both directions between the public and private domain. Firewalls are made of packet filters, proxy

---

services or a combination of both. Packet filters determine whether to forward a data packet by filtering IP addresses or TCP port numbers in the packet's header. It is the most economic of the solutions, offering excellent performance and transparency to applications, but it is a weak means of maintaining security. Proxy services do not allow traffic to pass directly, setting-up separate circuits to a server; they offer stronger security design but are inconvenient and offer poor transparency. Mixed approaches can either be a screened-host or a screen subnet design. Firewalls are specifically designed to protect against unauthorized access to Internet-linked networks. Several firewalls provide features such as network address translation, authentication, and virtual private networks (VPNs).

From an IT management perspective, there is no single product recommended for all security environments, but some stand out in particular circumstances. For example, Livingston Enterprises, Inc.'s Firewall IRX is identified in the trade press as a low-cost, entry-level offering. For large organizations that have restricted internal access, Internetwork Systems Corp.'s Security Router might be an appropriate choice. CheckPoint Software Technologies Ltd.'s Firewall-1 is a well-regarded product with an excellent management interface because it permits centralized configuration and administration of multiple firewalls. According to preliminary results from industry research firm IDC, CheckPoint Software Technologies, Ltd. is the market leader among commercial network security firewall vendors, with approximately 40% of the worldwide commercial firewall market in 1995.

The key issues in evaluating a security policy and firewall procedures should include the following:

- Identification and Authentication

- Privilege Control

- Confidentiality

- Application Security

- Physical Network Connections

There are many approaches to creating a firewall for the enterprise, but the most important issue is realizing the need for a firewall and performing the IT inventory assessment to determine what needs to be protected and how.

Internet Commerce

Today, commerce on the Internet is far from secure. Information is not comprehensively validated or protected, and security is not assured. From a security viewpoint, the medium itself gets in the way because people who are essentially anonymous, act differently than if they are face-to-face with a another person. Aside from authentication and authorization issues, ensuring transaction privacy and integrity is a concern. Items such as validation of order receipt and disputed billings handling are issues that must be addressed in the online security infrastructure that a potential Web merchant would build to offer products and services.

On the positive side, the Internet opportunities for commercial use are endless. As more computer users gain access, most observers agree that it is only a matter of time before the Internet lives up to its commercial potential. Forrester Research estimates this will happen in the next three years as Internet demographics even out and as merchants learn how to price and sell merchandise on the Web. However, most of the published demographic forecasts of these market research vendors only deal with the U.S. portion of commerce. In addition, some these U.S. merchants establishing pricing and shipping terms are just learning how to service foreign customers.

Before any potential can be achieved, a secure and flexible payment infrastructure must be devised by the merchant and its financial institution partners. According to IDC, "Until secure transactions can be guaranteed, Web sites will suffer the reputation of many browsers, few buyers, and very poor visit-to-buy ratios."

In this scenario, interoperability means an open, end-to-end payment transaction solution. This solution must consider all of the stages of a financial transaction and its security. These stages are:

- Authentication/Certification

- Authorization

- Secure Transmission

- Message Integrity

- Non-Repudiation

From the consumer perspective, requirements to perform transactions across the Internet include convenience, choice in payment options (credit, debt, stored-value cash, electronic cash, etc.), availability, security, and privacy. In the meantime, the merchant needs the assurances of payment, the consumer needs flexibility in payment options and the ability to avoid high fees or currency transaction costs. Financial institutions also need assurances geared by communication and message protocols, and strict security across the entire transaction.

While the issues of authentication and certification are being determined, a key answer to transaction security lies in public key encryption. The "smart card" solution, either a bank card or a special Internet "bank" card, provides a long-term remedy as a secure medium for holding specific information necessary for verification because only the public key needs to be transmitted across the network.

There are two other software protocols being considered for the implementation of Internet payment security, both of which are based on RSA Data Security (two encryption keys: One public, one private) encryption techniques:

- *S-HTTP (Secure HTTP):* This is an application-level protocol for the Web, developed by Enterprise Integration Technologies (EIT) and marketed by Terisa Systems, that provides privacy and digital signatures.

- *Server Side Includes (SSI)*: Developed by Netscape for privacy between the consumer and the merchant (the Web browser and the Web server). With these two competing approaches, server software providers are being urged by industry watchers to position themselves to support all the protocols offered.

Visa and Master Card are also working on a solution based on a new security protocol for electronic commerce. Given the influence these two organizations have in the market, they are likely to have a significant impact on electronic commerce in the longer term, and they will probably address all of the significant issues of online payment.

However, it is thought that software alone cannot address the entire security issue for online Internet commerce. Being limited to only using one's own PC on the Internet would be a factor in restricting trade, as would only being able to pay by credit card. Combined hardware and software solutions are the most effective and secure usage to date. For example, a new solution such as a bank card with a personal identification number (PIN). This card, used in a special machine at a retailer, can translate to a special card reader attached to the PC that has a unique bank card encrypted with a public and private software key. It is expected that hardware solutions will first penetrate the business procurement/purchasing applications and then migrate to home usage. This follows the pattern of Internet usage in general and Internet purchasing in particular.

There are no simple solutions to creating secure payment procedures for the Internet. However, the creation of an interoperable application layer of a combination of hardware and software to handle the functions and the standards that exist between the PC and Internet worlds make such a solution a short-term reality. Cooperation between vendors, financial institutions, and those with the knowledge of global payment needs will promote the proper payment environment for the future.

Choice of Internet Hardware

At present, users access the Internet through their PCs. However, many IT experts speculate that the "dumb" terminal will make a comeback as a low-cost Internet Access Device (IAD). Many industry leaders are investing time and resources in developing other methods of low-cost IAD – mainly in the under-$500 range – for home usage. Other access points could include television or hand-held computers. However, IT managers with heterogeneous hardware may be thinking of ways to utilize what is currently internally available to set-up more users with Internet connections.

A recent study by U.S. industry watcher IDC discussed the growth of these different IAD options through the year 2000. Figure 6.1 shows their forecasted data for this period for the following categories:

- *PCs:* General purpose PCs with Internet access.

- *Internet PCs:* Low-priced PCs (diskless or disk-limited) optimized for Internet access.

- *Internet terminals:* Terminal products optimized for Internet access.

- *Set-top boxes:* TV signal decoders with wireless remotes to access the Web through cable TV systems.

- *Digital Interactive Consumer Electronic (DICE) machines:* Videogames, digital video disk (DVD) players, CD-interactive (CD-I) players.

- *Other:* Devices such as lottery and gambling terminals, voting terminals, card readers, pagers, hand-held computers, and embedded systems.

Figure 6.1 Projected Worldwide Unit Shipments – Year 2000

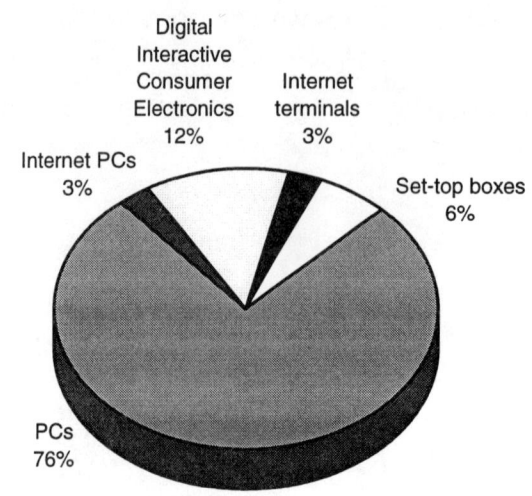

Source: IDC

IDC concluded the study with the opinion that each category of hardware was currently supported by a unique set of suppliers and a unique distribution infrastructure. Therefore the IAD market outside of PC systems will not interfere with PC sales for this purpose for at least the next five years. For the IT manager, this confirms the need for a common sense PC desktop strategy, rather than trying to convert terminals or other devices for unintended uses.

Choice of Internet Software

Internetscape, Microsoft, Sun, and Who Else?

With the various browsers, programming languages, and server offerings – especially in this burgeoning arena, making the decision on what (and who) to standardize on can be a confusing situation. Usually, one would start with either the established participant or the vendor with the most solid reputation. However, in this emerging market, an established vendor is difficult to locate. Microsoft, with its established software market presence, is late to the market; and the other companies and technologies can truly be called emerging, most within the last year. The recommendation from a standards point of view would be the Netscape browser from Internetscape Communications.

Marc Andreessen, co-founder of Internetscape Communications, sees The company's role as both a standards adopter and a setter of new standards. He notes that the Internet has always been based on open standards, although he admits products may move too fast for either network managers or end-users to keep pace. Andreessen says Microsoft products have many bugs and security holes, but the software giant is doing a great deal of work on security standards; his biggest problem with Microsoft is that its standards are not open. Internetscape's goal is not to replace desktop personal productivity applications because the company feels these are trivial compared to network applications.

Microsoft is following Internetscape's marketing devices by giving away copies of its browser – the Internet Explorer – with Windows 95 and Windows NT to establish market share. However, Netscape has a distinct advantage in the browser area in holding three-quarters of the currently estimated Internet browser market. Netscape has also created a plug-in API product so other applications can be used in conjunction with its browser, adding to the functionality. These plug-ins include an OLE control so users can embed OLE controls as applets in Navigator.

Microsoft is attempting to eliminate the need for browsers by adding browsing capabilities directly to Windows 95 through the Internet add-on it is expected to ship in late 1996, thus cutting back Netscape's market lead. In the future, Microsoft will add Internet access as a standard feature to both Windows NT and Windows 95.

Microsoft has also decided to support Java, the C++-based language developed at Sun Microsystems. Java produces applets that can work across networks and across platforms, and is rapidly taking off as a method of Internet application development. Microsoft, however, backed off from making their own tool set – Internet Studio (code name: Blackbird) – a proprietary system and based on Microsoft Network (MSN) alone. It will now function on the Internet without the proprietary MSN protocols. Microsoft has made a few blunders, such as MSN, in their quest to enter the cyberspace realm, but the company is known for quickly recovering from its troubles.

Netscape has a significant advantage in name recognition, setting Internet standards, and market share – factors with which Microsoft must now compete.

Intranet: The Internal Communication Device

According to IDC, more than 75% of all Web server software shipped in 1995 are being used for intranet servers, and by 1999, this number will grow to more than 91%. Many corporate MIS departments report they want to upgrade systems, even though the systems are still functioning. The desire to upgrade hinges on users frustrated at using character-based front-ends and the fact that many vendors will no longer upgrade critical components of core software services. One attractive option for corporate MIS departments is intranets, even though the intranets will not provide the same control level available with older systems. Intranets will truthfully never replace an entire system, but it will help MIS alter the way a firm does business and the way systems are developed. Application development will take weeks instead of years, and training to bring users online will be minimal. Web intranets are uncomplicated and feature a cross-platform client interface based on browsers currently in the marketplace.

Internet technology-based intranets are helping corporations find a simple means for providing employees access to important data. An intranet is a dedicated network that uses Web software to search a "mini-web" created solely for the company. The technology allows for a closed communications environment for offices, buildings or geographically dispersed branch offices. The tools needed to transform business documents into Web pages are inexpensive or free. The learning curve is low and information can be kept current, unlike printed manuals. Sun Microsystems, HP, and DEC all offer ready-to-plug-in, pre-configured Web servers for between $10,000 and $15,000.

Security is one of the best advantages of intranets, which are safe from the potential dangers of the Internet because they are protected behind the corporate firewall. Intranets, however, may be a two-edged sword. If information is power, intranets distribute power more evenly within a corporation.

The great thing about an intranet: It is easy-to-use and anyone can create or update content. There are, however, challenges to be faced, and questions to be answered: Should companies dictate the look-and-feel of every page or should users be given creative license? What additional intranet services such as interactive chatting should be offered? Who controls what is placed online? The power and flexibility of the intranet for distributing information at very low cost makes these minor obstacles. Management believes this type of activity increases productivity and efficiency; many companies are using intranets to anchor company communications. Web-based technology is inexpensive and easy-to-use and provides universal access to any employee with a Web browser. Analysts expect surging intranet server sales will outpace Internet server sales in the next three years as more companies embrace the technology (see figure 6.2).

Figure 6.2 Web Software Revenue

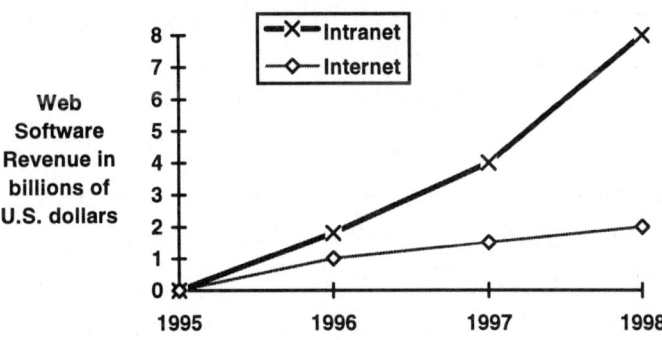

Source: Zona Research

Products designed specifically for intranets are already emerging; some are intended to replace traditional groupware by adding conferencing features to Internet servers. Internetscape Communications' purchase of Collabra Software is an obvious move toward such an intranet strategy. Other intranet products organize large corporate databases for viewing with a Web browser. Browser-based scripting languages allow the integration of many custom features into browsing technology.

The next step is the development of products based on Internet technology designed specifically for internal corporate use. This step is already happening. With tools designed to replace traditional groupware products.

Another emerging category involves products that organize many documents and make them available in a format that can be viewed with a Web browser. A third group of products are those designed to access large amounts of data; just about every maker of relational databases and database access tools is working on this capability.

The original idea was to use off-the-shelf browsers such as Internetscape Navigator, and most organizations will certainly proceed this way. Yet, many companies want to integrate browsing functionality with their own custom features.

When companies combine inexpensive browsers (with new collaboration and mail features) and browser-based scripting languages (whether Javascript or Visual Basic), suddenly one can create quite complex and powerful corporate applications based on Internet technology. This approach enables companies to use relatively inexpensive, field-tested tools and simultaneously migrate to the latest, hottest area of software: Internet products.

Already, groupware makers are rushing madly to make their products fit into an intranet solution. As a result, Lotus has cut the price on its Notes client and bundled Internet publishing tools with its Notes server. Novell is also adding to Groupwise features enabling companies to receive its mail through a Web browser.

Traditional groupware products continue to have a number of advantages. Some of these advantages are architectural such as Notes' ability to replicate seamlessly databases on multiple servers or even on clients. Others are implementation issues – products such as Notes and Groupwise have been around longer than many of the Internet-based collaboration products. Whether companies choose intranet or groupware technology, the bottomline is the same: Sharing information leads to better-informed employees, faster response times, and better customer relations.

Chapter 7

Information Management

The role of IS management has become strategic to the business enterprise as technology advances have added to its competitive positioning. A number of issues emerged as essential management considerations of the investment in IT and business strategy. Because IT transforms organizational boundaries, interorganizational relations, and the market positioning and competitive advantage of a company, its management requires a strategic level of control to optimize its advantages.

With more business-oriented responsibilities, IT management requires an integral view of how the use and maintenance of information occurs within the organization. This overview includes where data resides in the organization, the reuse of technology and information across the enterprise, and tools and strategies for developing common interfaces and implementations throughout the company. Effectively adopted information management is a prime enabler in meeting the growing number of new business challenges.

Data Sharing and Data Warehousing

All organizations possess data. The *volume* of data is not a problem most organizations would cite these days. The problem: Businesses have concentrated a large proportion of their resources (as much as 90% of the total IT budget during the last decade) into putting operational systems in place for collecting and holding data. Business are now looking for a discernible return on this investment.

Companies must determine what lies in mountains of indecipherable data stored on mainframes, minicomputers, and departmental servers.

Unfortunately, this also includes data that lies in standalone PCs and data of people who have left the company and have not correctly named files so others can decipher their content.

Two barriers must be overcome to make the data investment worthwhile:

1. Making data available

2. Providing data-hungry users a tool to locate the right information and then analyze it

Decentralization has opened a Pandora's box: Powerful servers have brought data within reach, and users are now clamoring to gain access. Glass-house MIS has responded by doing what it usually does: Large-scale application development and more custom reports. Unfortunately, this old approach does not work because it is expensive, slow, and assumes predictability and repetitiveness of questions.

This new generation of data-hungry users has evolved, similar to the change-hungry executives that Tom Peters calls "speedos" in his recent book, *Liberation Management*. Data-hungry users should have the following characteristics:

*   They need speed and they want to solve problems quickly

*   Their questions are unpredictable and rarely repeated

*   They are executives and managers, not data professionals

*   They use constant revolution and reinvention of the business as a means of beating competitors and increasing profit

Executive IS or decision support systems typically allow users to determine where a shipment is or how many parts were made last month. These "What is up?" queries do nothing more than ask predictable questions of highly structured data. There are many questions that cannot be asked: "Why is everything we ship through Houston late?" "What happened to Pacific Rim sales last month?" If these users can answer these questions and spot problems early, they can feed adjustments into the business process, thus improving company performance (see Figure 7.1). The kinetic feedback loop allows a company to react to the unpredictable questions that leads a company from asking the question "What went wrong?" to the question of "How can we make it better?"

Figure 7.1 The Data/Business Feedback Loop

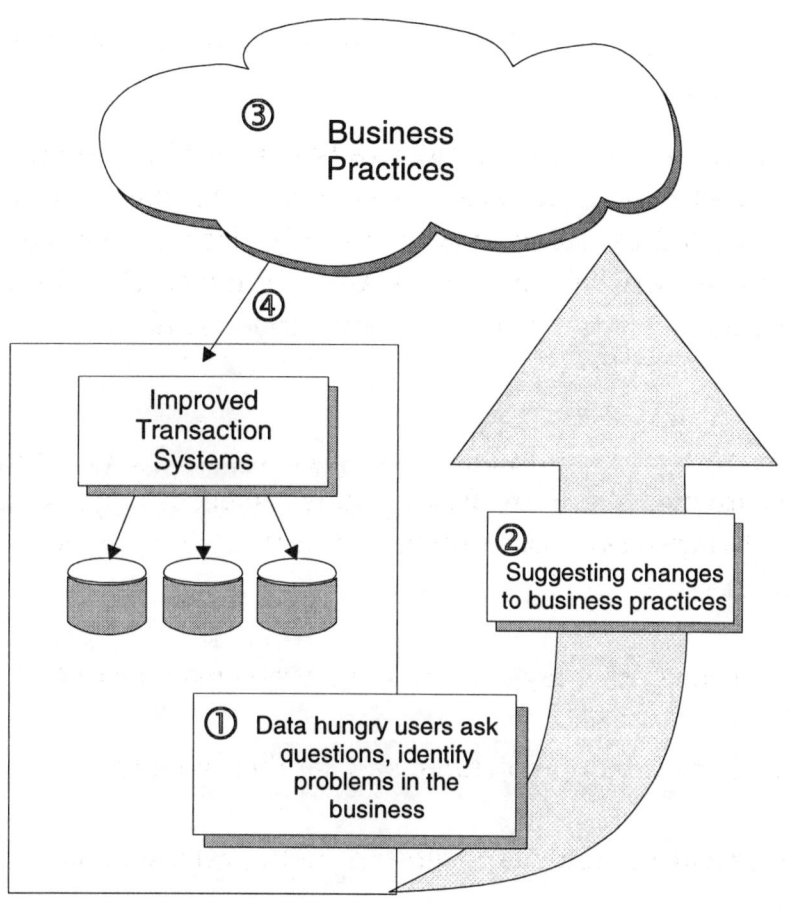

Forrester Research, Inc.

The ideal tool for this is what industry watchers call a "data drill." End-users with varying levels of expertise want to ask the questions that will enable them to perform their jobs and they do not want anyone looking over their shoulders while they do it. The "data drill" will be characterized by three features:

1. *Easy to learn and use:* The tools will use GUIs and SQL statement builders to hide complex database structures, allowing non-technical

---

users to point-and-click their way to the data they need. The tools must scale from simple inquiry to complex data analysis.

2. *Broad support for data sources:* The tools must provide access to all popular server and host databases.

3. *Minimal or no MIS involvement:* Some MIS involvement such as access control, download scheduling will be necessary, but the less interaction with MIS, the better.

In short, users want a powerful, versatility, and simple data-drill. Today's data access tools do not quite reach this performance level. Although they do offer support for a broad variety of databases, they require a sophisticated user and a high level of MIS support.

Today's data-drills can be segmented into three major categories:

1. *Query and report:* Ad hoc query tools, such as Formula OpenSoft's QBEVision, let users retrieve data from a server database and report writers, such as Indigo's ReportSmith, and format the data into reports. Both query and report tools insulate users from the vagaries of SQL syntax and semantics but not from detailed knowledge of data tables and relational joins.

2. *Slice-and-dice:* Investigative analysis tools such as Cognos' PowerPlay turn data savvy users into detectives. Users such as accountants, marketing directors, and customer service experts can burrow into the data in ways their intimate knowledge of the data uniquely qualifies them to do. Slice-and-dice tools are most effectively used by people who understand both the business problem and the data structures.

3. *Develop and deploy:* IS development tools such as Channel Computing's Forest & Trees allow users to turn regular queries into low-cost, easily maintainable and easily modifiable departmental IS. Without PC-experienced, data savvy users, these development tools are useless.

The current data access tools offer too wide a variety of capabilities. The industry vendors are unable to offer any compelling differentiation from each other and even from mainstream products. For example, database products such as Microsoft Access perform many of the same functions as today's data access products. C/S power tools such as PowerBuilder and SQLWindows also provide options. The major differentiator and the goal is to enable professional developers to quickly build industrial-strength, transaction-oriented applications.

Inappropriate design is not the only reason data access tools have not become more popular. Structural and organizational problems also stand in the way:

- *The data infrastructure is all wrong:* Transaction data is structured to make life easy for COBOL programmers, not for business users. Non-intuitive field names and highly normalized tables conspire to make data inaccessible to most users. To make data accessible to the people who need it, data must be transformed into a more usable shape and combined with pertinent local and corporate data.

- *Central MIS owns the resources to make it work:* Data facilities need somebody who understands the data and can communicate this understanding to other users. Departments do not have this kind of person on staff, but central MIS does. Yet MIS is concerned with loss of central control and security, skeptical about the tools and methodologies, and fearful of runaway queries.

- *Enabling technologies are too new:* Open database APIs such as Microsoft's ODBC, Borland's Integrated Database Application Programming Interface (IDAPI), and Information Builder's EDA/SQL allow access to every data source but are only now on their way to broad acceptance. Brand new data transfer engine technologies Redbrick's Goldmine, Channel Computing's InfoPump, and Sybase's Replication Server will allow IT organizations to regularly download data from a wide variety of production databases into more usable forms.

Given the serious infrastructural, political, and technological problems, users will require better tools such as "data drills" and less confusion about the tool usage in the future. If product consolidation takes place, Forrester Research estimates the 1997 market for data drills could be between $700 and $900 million in size.

As "data drill" usage grows, the need for an improved data infrastructure will push the MIS department toward solutions that incorporate a combination of:

- Server databases such as Sybase and Oracle

- Data transfer engines such as Channel's InfoPump

- Widespread adoption of open database APIs such as ODBC and EDA/SQL

- The use of systems integrators, both from central MIS and from companies such as Cambridge Technology Partners

The benefits of enhanced data access will improve the link between technology and profitable business. Several benefits stand out:

- *The feedback loop will become entrenched:* The use of a data drill to determine a business process is wrong, then changes to the business practice will improve the way the organization works. It will speed internal business changes and reengineering efforts.

- *Legacy applications will fade faster:* As business and market pressures accelerate the decision-making process, old-line decision support and EIT products will become less relevant. Companies will move the decision systems off mainframes onto more flexible systems based on C/S networks. Legacy applications will be less appropriate choices for the business model in use.

- *Decentralization of IT functions will continue:* As companies push an increasing amount of responsibility from centralized IT functions to business units, these groups will have access to data they need. Lines of business will become more capable manipulators of the data they understand better than anyone else.

Data warehousing, as recognized by the major industry hardware and software suppliers, is probably the most significant development to hit the IT industry for many years and is forecast to grow dramatically at a rate of 65% per year, according to market estimates. Data warehousing addresses the issues of organizing, managing, and exploiting data while allowing companies to protect their IT investments. Coupled with the task of unlocking data is the challenge of the competitive business world, leading to the consolidation of key business data needs into these areas: Finance, production, sales and marketing, and distribution. Because of the informational needs to turn operational data into business decisions, data has to be managed from all business sources, both internal and external to the organization. The data warehouse concept gives the opportunity for decision makers to prepare integrated pictures of the business using cross-organizational data summarized for decisions (see figure 7.2).

Figure 7.2 A Data Warehousing Model

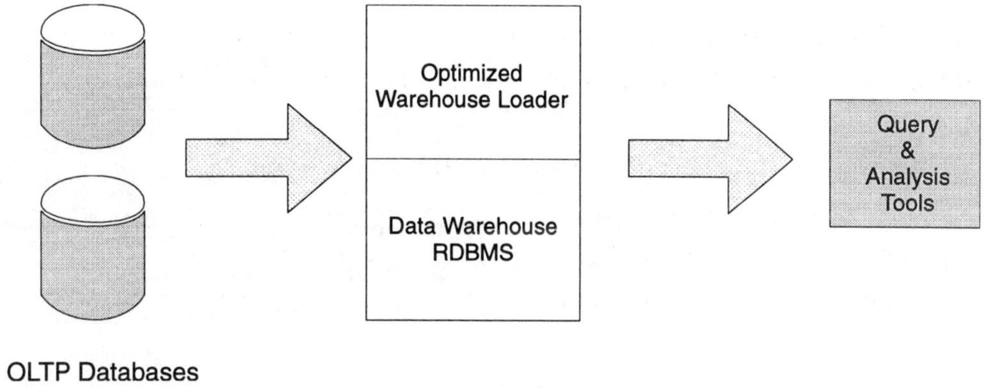

OLTP Databases

The data warehouse concept evolved from the growing competitive needs to quickly analyze business information. Existing operational systems cannot meet this need because:

- There is a lack of online historical data

- Data required for analysis resides in different operational systems

- Extremely poor query performance affects the performance of operational systems

- Operational database designs are inappropriate for decision support

As with "data drills," data warehouses are infrastructural constructions to be used when commercial forces make organizations face the restructuring issues that involve both IT and the business objectives. Data warehouses, as shown in Figure 7.2, are a combination of historical data accessed by a database engine and loading/cleansing tools, with a front-end solution encompassing query and analysis products, whether it be spreadsheets or SQL tools. The most politically charged portion of this access is the query tools, because for the most part, they are what the uses see on the desktop and how they interact with the warehouse. Query tools must be user-friendly, thus putting pressure on developers to put the more sophisticated development into the warehouse itself, and leave the query tools simple and easy.

The hype surrounding the data warehousing phenomena is based on the C/S craze and users' needs to access "legacy" data in proprietary systems which are generally not network accessible. In the future, financial systems or business software suites will offer the same functionality data warehouses are now touting. Users need the data now, but designing custom reports is becoming too costly an approach to continue using. Providing an intermediary measure with data mining tools and data "cleansing" operations – that remove, for example, low-level transaction information to make the operational data more easily accessible – are necessary steps to provide a more dynamic data environment for the end-user. Within the next 18 months, package suites for data warehousing may be available. In the meantime, however, data warehousing and its associated issues is one of the key methodologies for data sharing.

Cross-Organizational Software Reuse

Software reuse is the practice of using existing software components to develop new applications. Reusable software components can be executable programs, code segments, documentation, requirements, design and architectures, test data, and test plans or software tools. They may also be knowledge and information needed to understand, develop, use or maintain the component.

Software reuse is beneficial if a company do it, but most organizations do not. The best MIS groups are consistently achieving reuse levels of 70% to 80%, and occasionally reaching levels as high as 95%. Typical MIS shops are only reusing 20% to 30% of existing code. The real problem: Most shops are not reusing any software. Why not? Because software text books do not teach it, the "not invented here" syndrome keeps developers from using others' code, older and less mature reuse technologies scared some early practitioners away, and there are no incentives for developers to reuse code in most IT shops.

Developing and maintaining software in organizations is very costly. According to many experts in the software community, software reuse is a possible solution to reduce these costs and increase software productivity and reliability. Although these benefits and savings are compelling, achieving them will require the resolution of significant technical, organizational, and legal issues.

Even while proclaiming the reuse potential, many software experts have questioned the maturity of software reuse. These experts indicate methodologies to implement reuse have not been fully developed, tools to support a reuse process are lacking, and standards to guide critical software reuse activities have not been established.

Beyond such technical difficulties, organizations also face numerous challenges to effectively implement and practice software reuse. An organization must make a significant commitment to reuse because fundamental changes in the organization's software development approach will be needed and significant initial costs for training and tools will be required. Further, uncertainties in legal policies such as liability and intellectual property rights that currently hinder software reuse must be addressed, and acquisition policies must be modified to better promote reuse. Figure 7.3 shows examples of the different types of reusable software components.

Figure 7.3 Examples of Reusable Software Components

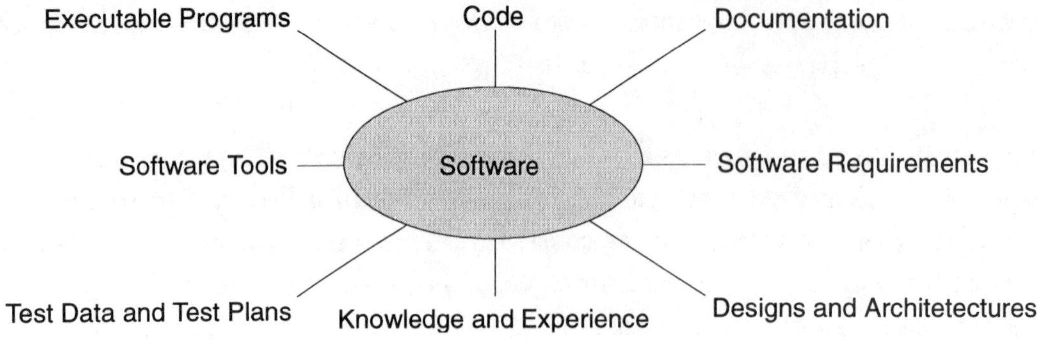

Source: U.S. Department of Defense

This framework, established by the U.S. Defense Advanced Research Projects Agency's (DARPA) Software Technology for Adaptable Reliable Systems (STARS) program, presents the flow of information within the software reuse process and its products. The U.S. government has been a forerunner in the area of software reuse research.

In defining software reuse, one can look at it in two basic forms:

1. Opportunistic

2. Systematic

Opportunistic reuse is practiced in an ad-hoc fashion during software development. In opportunistic reuse, new applications are developed from software that has been salvaged from existing systems and modified to meet the specific needs of that application. Systematic reuse is planned and integrated into a well-defined software development process. In systematic reuse, new applications are developed from software designed and developed to be reused specifically for other similar applications.

In systematic reuse, new reusable software is also created as a by-product of applications development. The software reuse process consists of three stages: Component creation, component management, and component utilization. Software reuse can be practiced vertically or horizontally. Vertical reuse is the reapplication of software components within a single domain. For example, a software component that implements procedures to withdraw taxes from a paycheck can be reused by different accounting systems within the payroll application domain. Horizontal reuse, on the other hand, is the reuse of software components across different domains. For example, software components such as sort and merge procedures, can be reused by systems in many application domains.

A domain is a family of related systems that exhibit common objects and operations. Domain analysis involves systematically gathering and representing information on software applications. Experts in the software community generally agree domain analysis is the "heart of reuse." Its purpose is to generalize common features in similar application areas, identify the common objects and operations in these areas, and describe their relationships. Once collected, the information can be used to create reusable software components that support these areas. For example, in an airline reservation system domain, common objects are flights and seats, while common operations include flight scheduling and seat assignments. These objects and operations are related in specific ways to the airline reservation system domain. As such, software components that support these objects and operations could be reused by developers of other airline reservation systems.

Domain analysis is a complex process that involves acquiring and representing knowledge on specific domains. Information on the domain must be identified, compiled, analyzed, and represented in a format so it can be reused. The domain analyst must not only identify the objects, operations, and their relationships in the domain, but also explicitly represent that information so others can easily understand and reuse it.

However, standard methods to process and represent information on a domain are lacking. Current domain analysis methodologies such as the Software Engineering Institute's feature-oriented domain analysis (FODA), are still evolving, and thus, do not completely address these functions.

During component creation, domains where reuse is possible are identified and reusable software components are developed. Once components are developed, they are stored and managed in a software repository, which is a library that allows users to access, search, and retrieve the components. Key functions of component management include certifying, classifying, and cataloguing components, and configuration control of the software components as a result of software upgrades and maintenance.

The benefits of software reuse are not easily or quickly realized. The potential impact of software reuse remains questionable because of technical, organizational, and legal issues that must be addressed. Establishing a systematic software reuse program is difficult. Few organizations in either the private or public sectors have been able to incorporate software reuse into their software development practices because the technical knowledge to develop and apply software reuse methodologies, standards, and tools is still evolving.

Interoperability is an important capability in instances where multiple repositories exist because it permits software repositories to share components, reduce the number of redundant components in the different repositories, and make components available to all repository users. Development is currently under way, for example, in DARPA's STARS program to establish an architectural framework for repository interoperability. However, interoperability standards of software repositories such as nomenclature, communication protocols, and component exchange formats do not exist. Currently, the Reuse Library Interoperability Group (RIG) is addressing standards for interoperability and plans to submit proposals to standards organizations such as the IEEE.

Interoperability by software reuse can also be attempted by adaptation, which is modifying a software component to make it reusable in different software applications. The software developer must determine what interfaces are needed and then integrate the components. Because the current state-of-practice is mainly opportunistic, most of the benefits that can be gained from software reuse are highly dependent on effective adaptation methods. However, adaptation is a difficult process because the developer must understand how the component currently functions, how the new application works, and what modifications are needed to make the component work in the new application.

Without this information, a developer cannot easily adapt the software component for reuse. Even with the information, the adaptation process can be labor-intensive, potentially off-setting time and cost savings promised from software reuse.

Although the current software reuse state-of-practice has been limited to the code reuse, experts believe the reuse of other software products, such as systems designs and architectures, can further increase the benefits of software reuse. They call this "higher level reuse" because it involves reusing products from software development phases that occur prior to (or higher than) the one in which code is written. According to these experts, the reuse of higher level components will yield greater benefits because designs and architectures are more flexible than code. The reason: Higher level components are independent of language, hardware platforms, and implementation-specific details, and represent application solutions rather than implementation solutions; RIG is a volunteer organization composed of members from government, academia, and private industry. Membership is open to any organization interested in the interoperability of government-sponsored reuse libraries.

In the traditional software development process, there are four successive phases: Planning, design, coding and testing, and integration and testing. However, formally representing systems designs and architectures in a reusable form is very difficult because they are not as tangible as code. Further, standards and tools to represent and develop systems designs and architectures are lacking. Therefore, software metrics may be useful to determine the measurement of software reuse success.

Software Metrics

Software metrics are quantifiable measures used to assess the products and processes of software development. Such metrics may include measures of usefulness, cost, and quality that could be used to better manage software development programs. However, identifying and establishing metrics is difficult because standard methodologies do not exist to collect data for software development and products in general or for reuse in particular. As such, current metrics are inconsistent, metrics interpretation can vary from individual to individual, and collecting metrics is a very expensive and time-consuming process.

Without effective metrics, however, organizations cannot adequately determine the costs and benefits of incorporating software reuse into their software development processes. Software reuse will not happen merely because the technical means for achieving it become available. Software experts agree top management must be convinced to make a business decision to incorporate systematic reuse into the software development process. Further, project managers and software developers must be willing to make fundamental changes in the way they develop software. Otherwise, software reuse will remain at the opportunistic level, and the potentially greater benefits of systematic reuse will not be realized.

Committing to Software Reuse

For a software reuse program to be successful, top management must decide and commit to implementing a systematic reuse program throughout the organization. Top management must incorporate software reuse practices into the software development process, train and educate employees on software reuse, develop and provide tools to practice software reuse, and allocate the proper funds and resources to support a reuse program.

Some believe top management is hesitant to invest in software reuse because the benefits of software reuse are not quickly realized and are uncertain. To illustrate, some experts estimate the savings from reusing a component will not be realized until that component has been reused at least three times and believe it initially costs about 20% to 55% more to develop reusable software.

Another common organizational issue is the unwillingness of project managers and software developers to design and reuse components. Developing reusable software is more costly and time-consuming. As such, project managers, often pushed by limited funds and tight schedules, have little incentive to allocate the additional time and resources needed to develop reusable software components.

Additionally, software developers are often reluctant to accept and use reusable components for fear the components will not be as efficient, effective or reliable as the software they write. Further, using reusable software components requires the components be understood and adapted to meet the specific needs of a software system before it can be integrated. In either case, the reluctance of software developers to use reusable software and the lack of incentives for program managers to develop reusable software components remain issues that must be addressed.

Software Reuse Legal Issues

The software community's hopes for widespread reuse also brings about a number of challenging legal issues. Software patents and licensing policies must be addressed. Reuse experts believe strategies are needed to address intellectual property rights, liability, and acquisition policies of reuse. Software is protected legally as intellectual property through laws that control its dissemination and use. These laws relate to the exclusive ownership of the idea, the form of expression of the idea, and the use of the idea and its expression.

There are three basic methods to protect software: Patents, copyrights, and trade secrets. Patents protect the rights to the idea itself, while copyrights protect the rights to the expression of the idea. Trade secret laws protect the rights to confidential business information. However, in many cases, laws are unclear about the enforcement of intellectual property rights. As such, a major challenge facing software reuse is to balance these rights between software suppliers, repositories, and users.

There is an overall need to promote the value of reuse across the organization. IT managers must show the return on investment, how the company can increase its productivity, add to its efficiency, reduce development lead times, implement changes more quickly, and finally, reduce the software operating and maintenance costs. There is also a need to explain interpreting software metrics to management, and vendors must be encouraged to produce sufficient software products as future priorities necessary to reuse components later.

Storage Management: Proactive Efficient Strategies

Storage devices are becoming a commodity product, although this is not a new concept according to storage resellers. However, this does not change the important factors in cost of ownership such as ease-of-installation, maintenance charges, usage management, and compatibility with future platforms. There are several issues to consider when implementing a companywide storage management strategy – the first being to actually have a strategy.

Most users now operate in a multivendor environment, which creates a number of management and integration issues. Shopping for the end-user's needs is a tempting concept when and if storage products are required. However, this approach often leads to inefficient use of existing storage, with some platforms having considerable amounts of spare capacity, while other operate with the bare minimum. This approach also tends to encourage the purchase of proprietary products for each platform, incurring high initial costs and inflated maintenance charges. Purchasing proprietary products is sufficient for smaller users with a low overall investment and a less steep growth path, but if the system disk on the server goes out leaving 50 users idle, the company's IT department has a problem on its hands.

Through the 1990s, the requirements for storage have soared, primarily due to the needs of the application software market, where every application from GUI to multimedia has placed increasing demands on processing and storage systems. Responding to the need for better backup and storage, data protection and management technologies are transforming into increasingly sophisticated solutions.

The old adage "time does not stand still" is particularly poignant in the storage management arena. Data management has historically taken many different forms, from simple duplication of files to storage media, for example, tape backup systems to completely mirrored file servers that can transparently take over operations in the event of a primary file server failure.

Tape backup systems and software have typically migrated from workstation-based systems to file server-based ones, resulting in improved performance due to the use of file server bus speeds instead of serial network speeds. LAN administrators have generally configured tape operations to occur during off-hours (generally at night) to ensure all protected files are closed and properly backed-up. As the volume of data has grown, higher-capacity tape systems and faster transfer rates have evolved to meet changing backup needs.

Even with these performance enhancements, file-by-file backup is still becoming more difficult. The amount of stored data is increasing too quickly, making it nearly impossible to perform complete backups during off hours, when users are logged off and files are closed. In addition, many systems are now operating mission-critical applications that cannot be shut down, and therefore, cannot be effectively backed up and protected from loss.

Mission-critical application servers are often configured with mirrored disks, duplexed disks or rapid array of inexpensive disk (RAID) subsystems to further protect the data they hold and to provide a high percentage of application availability to end-users. High-end solutions such as mirrored servers have evolved to supply 100% availability; combined with tape backup systems, these solutions provide an even higher degree of protection for mission-critical data.

Another result of the growing volume of data has been the migration of infrequently accessed data to near-line storage systems such as optical servers. This solution represents the continuing effort to free storage capacity on the main-line, high-speed, direct-access storage disks that must be used for frequently accessed data. File-by-file backup systems have carried the load for a long time, but the burdens of increasing amounts of data and limits surrounding suitable backup times have pushed for alternative solutions.

Storage management systems that utilize new technologies to combine decentralized and centralized computing and storage techniques provide businesses with competitive advantages. IT managers need data storage systems that provide data security, can share data, have fast response times, are user-friendly, and cost-effective. A wide variety of storage systems are available, including Static Random Access Memory (SRAM), Dynamic Random Access Memory (DRAM), solid state Direct Access Storage Device (DASD), automated tape libraries, and manual tape systems. The type of technology selected for data storage is critical to a an organization's success. Technologies such as virtual volume management and automated tape cartridges can vastly improve an enterprise's ability to access information. Implementing a paperless office system (as much as humanly possible) is another method that can improve efficiency and save an organization money.

Successful organizations are painfully aware of what the information age entails. Record storage is no longer simply a library of historical records. Electronically available data serves as the preprocess reservoir for a transformation that yields vital information in a highly competitive marketplace. How can a company keep the data close enough to meet business objectives that still make economic sense?

In taking advantage of new technologies, companies realize that change is a constant, and modification of IT operations and implementations results in many benefits. Assorted applications (caused by the various reasons for consolidation) create the impetus to acquire remote work group procedures. Disaster avoidance, a natural follow-on to a consolidation, may be the stimulus to propose vaulting. Applications such as journaling and logging to tape, which keep track of changes in a database, are critical for resiliency of online changes to a database. Captures of a DASD farm are critical for the restoration of operating systems, applications, and data. The captured data may never be used again unless there is a disaster, but it is so critical there is no question as to whether it is necessary.

Businesses that do not give consideration to basic data management and recovery may face an IT disaster when a widespread network/computer disruption occurs. Storage administrators must perform backup and restore procedures, and implement policies to address the absence of storage management. Procedures can be established concerning removable media management, data security, disaster recovery procedures, and capacity planning. Storage administrators can also prepare for a disaster by backing up data and shipping it off site.

Several types of local backup are available such as backup to tape, optical jukeboxes, mirrored servers, and automated tape libraries. Storage administrators should select backup tape products based on their cost and ability. Although backup and restore procedures are only one aspect of reliable storage management, they are critical to managing a distributed system.

If one harbors any doubts about storage management problems characterized by out-of-control management, disk-space problems, and manual archiving consider this: According to Strategic Research Corp. of Santa Barbara, California, out of the $350,000 a U.S. corporation typically spends for LAN storage and management, 28% represents productivity lost due to downtime and lack of performance, while 41% actually goes to disk and file management; the remaining 31% is a combination of infrastructural costs, including server and other types of hardware, bandwidth, and software programs.

According to storage hardware vendors, network software developers, users, and analysts, the steep price – both in dollars and man-hours – has propelled the emergence of a network-industry niche; one intent on providing software-based storage management solutions. Of these solutions, none has generated a bigger buzz than hierarchical storage management (HSM).

HSM systems and software vendors are releasing new products that capitalize on the growing desire among network managers for increased network storage capacity and control. In typical network configurations, approximately 69% of all expenses go to productivity downtime cost and disk and file administration. HSM software is designed to reduce that cost. It automatically monitors the capacity of hard disks and organizes the transference of data and files between magnetic disks to optical disks to tapes, based on pre-established criteria. The HSM software market remained at a relatively low $33 million earning level in 1995, primarily because of a lack of information by network managers and inconsistent features in products. However, analysts expect the market to grow substantially in conjunction with improved understanding and products. Figure 7.4 examines the data storage hierarchy from a performance/cost basis.

Figure 7.4 Data Storage Hierarchy

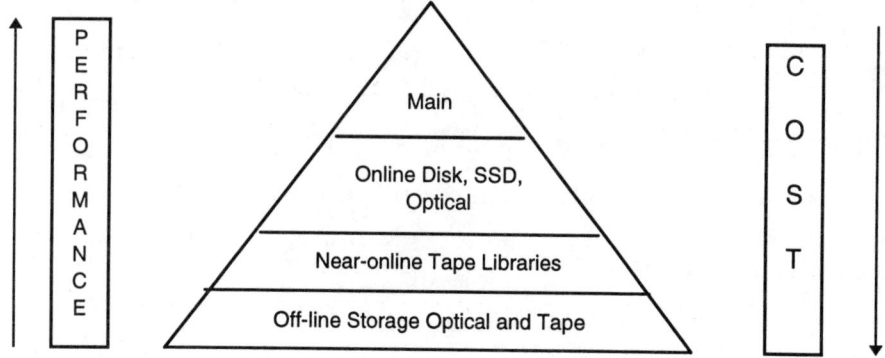

Reliable backup and restore provisions are only a small part of enterprise storage management. The technology exists today to establish consistent levels of data availability on heterogeneous platforms and systems across the enterprise. This is an important first step to take in distributed systems management. The risks many organizations are taking with critical data that is time-consuming and expensive to recreate are simply unacceptable. If the organization is still considering enterprise storage management rather than something different, it is probably time the IT department working on a solution.

Graphical Frontiers in Print Management

An IT strategy that covers more than data processing and follows corporate information all the way to the end-user, will preclude unnecessary output expenses. If the company does not have a printing strategy, it will usually buy whatever happens to be on the market at the lowest price. If the company does not do this, it may probably trip over another trap it can fall into without a plan: Application-specific printers.

A line printer is purchased because it can handle three-part paper, and that is what the application requires. Then a high-quality laser printer is bought to print letters. Neither device is constantly busy, and neither device can fill in for the other. A sound printer strategy would consider a single, flexible device that is busy most of the time, rather than two single-purpose printers that spend a great deal of time idle.

Formulating a sound output strategy is no different than any other kind of IT planning. Questions must be asked about what business the company is active in, where it is headed, and how technology can best help it get there. When it comes to printing, the question here is: Where in the enterprise does the printing need to occur? With everything from the desktop to the traditional glass house connected, there are unlimited choices. The choice could be printing financial reports, for example, to locked mailboxes on distributed printers throughout the network. Another choice could also be to produce the company's monthly billing at regional centers across the country.

Another important issue is the amount of graphics required in documents throughout the enterprise, whether it is a financial document or a company presentation. Even today's memos include graphics, which leads to the issue of choosing a color printer or a monotone printer. In most organizations, the answer has been ultimately color because these prices have decreased and the need for color has dramatically increased.

With competition rising, costs soaring, and data moving throughout the enterprise more easily than ever, it is no wonder many companies are looking beyond the desktop lasers and the glass house printers for efficient, effective output. One area many companies find increasingly appealing is the midrange bracket of network printers, with a range of 20 pages per minute (ppm) to 50 ppm.

Analysts agree that, while currently, the fast laser-quality printing segment is small, it is fast-growing. What would make one consider a printer in this class rather than a legion of laser printers? Maybe mainframe use is dwindling and the company is becoming more geographically distributed, in which case a user may require a desktop printer because they are unable to retrieve print-outs in a timely manner from a central printing location.

Further, a company may need a device that can print several hundred thousand pages per month on a fairly wide variety of paper sizes and types. A printer such as this could handle many of the output needs of a fairly large department, taking a strain off the mainframe printer and desktop printers alike.

A departmental printer can do more than pick up parts of the existing workload. Perhaps its biggest appeal is the freedom it gives to rethink the entire print paradigm. Print-on-demand is a good example. Rather than printing large volumes of paper – in the cases of employee handbooks or benefits manuals for instance – in a central location, then shipping them and storing them on shelves until they are needed. Why not store those documents electronically. Update them as often as necessary; when users at a particular location need one or more copies of the document, they can print it locally.

If IT can print more than 25,000 pages per month on a large printer, management will probably be satisfied in terms of cost. The cost per page and the total cost of ownership of a departmental printer is going to be noticeably less at that volume (and at higher volumes) than it would be using only desktop printers.

One of the more important points to consider when buying printers is software: Software embedded in the printer's controller, software for managing print jobs, and software that integrates printing as part of the workflow. Printer controllers are a very crucial issue. A buyer will want to ask the seller if the controller's programming is flexible and whether it can be upgraded easily. One should also consider whether the processor on the board is fast enough to handle the most complex jobs.

QMS, Inc. of Mobile, Alabama is a leader in this area because it has very powerful controllers based on its Crown technology. A high-powered RISC processor allows Crown to run a UNIX kernel and provide management capabilities: Queuing jobs, reporting on the printer's status, even reconfiguring the printer for a particular environment or a particular job.

Rethinking the printing paradigm can yield beneficial results for efficiency and competitiveness, but these advantages come at a cost. Exploiting a departmental printer's capabilities means more software is needed: Queue managers, forms managers, and document management libraries. Some may come with the printer, but the software must fit the company's situation so one might be prepared to find third-parties that can cover the missing or inadequate software functions.

Accurately justifying printer management strategy requires a clear understanding of costing and sizing elements. Besides amortizing the purchase price, the calculation must include the total cost per page based on the overall ownership and operation costs of a particular printer as it relates to an organization's mix of hard-copy output, the printer's duty cycle, (the number of pages it can print in a month, which varies with the type and quantity of output), speed, consumables, and support for multiple schemes and service.

When implementing printer management, consider the overall solution for the enterprise and beyond the individual user needs. Everyone wants a printer on or near their desk, but the reality for the company is the best solution overall, not *for* all.

Tools for Systems Management

In the mainframe days, one could use CICS to manage everything – throughput, performance, and applications – from a centralized location. With distributed C/S applications, managing from a central location can be very difficult. Especially if the company has different networks, different databases, different operating systems, and vastly different applications and user groups. The current systems management goal is to obtain the end-to-end view while maintaining costs. The cost factor is definitely critical, according to the Gartner Group, because organizations are spending twice as much to manage C/S applications than it took to manage centralized, mainframe-based applications.

Both companies and systems management vendors understand the problem that needs solving. Administrators need a logical view of the network such as the ability to associate resources (including human resources) with a particular application and the ability to invoke a variety of management functions such as security, network monitoring and alarms, trouble-ticketing, software distribution, and asset management to keep that application running smoothly. Open Systems Research, a New York City systems management research firm, defines the application management scenario in this manner. According to them, no vendor yet has the ability to provide such a complete, logical management solution. Vendors have at least agreed on three technology enablers necessary to present users with a unified view across the enterprise:

1. *Object-oriented architectures*: Object-oriented GUIs can enable managers to encapsulate hardware, software, users, and processes into classes represented by icons. Data can be stored so it is associated with objects and can be called logically by invoking an object. Communications can be object-enabled, so that processes can invoke one another based on logically defined policies.

2. *Agent technology:* Vendors are attempting to distribute management processes while keeping control centralized. Agent technology allows this to happen. Agents can be coded into applications and/or incorporated into network devices to collect information and relay it back to the management application. Intelligent agents take this one step further by interpreting management data and performing corrective actions at a local level, then notifying a central management station or trouble-ticketing application of problems or activity.

3. *Central repository:* Applications must store network, hardware, and software information in a common repository. By pulling data from the repository, management applications can provide administrators and

managers with different views, depending on the tasks they are performing.

A variety of existing systems management products feature object-oriented GUIs. A growing number of vendors are working with tool and application vendors to build intelligent agents into their products to make them more manageable. Fewer vendors are attempting to build a complete systems management architecture – from the ground up – based on a common management repository. The complete picture of systems management for today's enterprise is still a bit far off, but users are optimistic and suppliers have realized the challenges and cost justifications necessary to provide solutions for companies facing these issues.

Cross-Organization Commonalties

A common approach to the structure and management of information and technology in an organization is necessary. Starting at the desktop, commonalties across the organization, in the long-run, save money and time. Specific areas of interests to the IT manager are:

- *Common User Interface:* A similar look-and-feel at every desktop. This focuses on the user responding in the same way to the same stimulus. The major issue is ease-of-use; if users do not like the interface, they will not use it.

- *Common Process Integration:* More of an issue from the enterprise level, process reengineering is a very popular IT topic and is one of the key elements of restructuring the IT software business. Simplicity is the most important aspect: Difficulty, cost, and risk increases as complexity increases.

- *Common Data Repository:* A major concern, especially in the data warehouse craze of the 1990s. Users see the mainframe's future as a data server/repository, but with networking issues and heterogeneous environments, few people agree on where data should be housed.

- *Common Event Reporting:* An issue more for systems and network management, this allows users to generate reports on events or data that occurred within a specific period of time. As data sources become more regularized, methodologies for event reporting will also become more standardized.

Commonalties will occur more frequently as the hardware and communications aspects of IT management become more integrated, which will be driven by the user community pushing vendors to become more standardized in their approach.

From an internal point of view, having cross-organizational standards across business units and across acquired companies is a challenge many are trying to meet on a tactical basis. The key is to be proactive, not reactive, and put into place a buying strategy and a development policy that underscores the importance of common interfaces and common usage.

In summary, information management involves taking advantage of the commonalties available within the organization's IT structure, and standardizing the aspects that simplify the process of utilizing information.

Chapter 8

Resource Needs

In an increasingly competitive world, IT managers must focus their limited resources on the companies' core business, and IT staffing is not generally part of that mandate. While outsourcing some of the IT support makes sense, it also causes concern. Having the company's "internals," including core business processes and company secrets, potentially available to an "outsider" can cause complications at the senior management level.

In this dynamic market, "let the buyer beware" should be the watchword of the day because outsourcers, consultants, system integrators, even computer vendors are falling all over each other to offer integration and other IT services to the end-user community.

As technology becomes more complicated and IT department numbers decline, many companies look to off-load at least some of their end-user support. Almost half of 1,000 of the companies responding to a survey from the Help Desk Institute say they currently outsource help desk support, and is another 25% plan to do so this year. Where there is demand, there will be a surge of supply. The outsourcing market is becoming crowded, not only with providers specializing in support, but also with the rest of the IT industry jumping into what they expect to be an extremely lucrative business.

Internal resources are also an issue. For IT, business contribution can now be seen as more important than technical knowledge. The face of computing has changed. Business acumen is now the primary requirement for most professionals. Technical skills must add value to the business. Increased competition, privatization, facilities management, dynamic networks, and business reorganization has brought everyone closer to the customer. This has not been a comfortable process for many in the IT world.

Many company quality standards now require that, whatever function anyone in a business undertakes, they do it for a customer, internal or external. The satisfaction of that customer is then the paramount concern. Computer-based IS are being geared to serve business functions. The closed development environment created by the existence of IS and data processing departments as separate entities has never been successful. It simply created a barrier between end-users and computing resource controllers.

The future and productivity of the IT department resources lies in a more open view of IT development, with end-users and developers as partners in the process and third-party services viewed as an extension of the IT department itself.

Outsourcing Expertise Can Be Expensive

Outsourcing continues to be an increasingly viable option for large and medium sized companies. IDC predicts the global outsourcing market in the year 2000 to exceed $121 billion, with a compound annual growth rate of 10% (see Figure 8.1).

Figure 8.1 Global Outsourcing Market

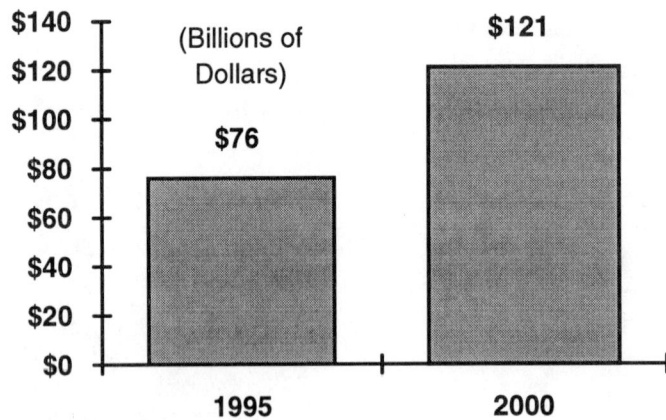

Source: IDC

Issues driving this market growth include increased competition in the field and the focus on business core competencies which causes IT managers to

---

consider outsourcing many of their IT operations. However, because of competition, the global outsourcing market model is evolving to a model where the outsourcer becomes more of a long-term business partner in an attempt to create value and increase profit margin.

With this marketplace evolution, the type of assistance one can receive from an outsourcing company will change from the traditional gap-filling or migrating systems role to a position where expertise is taught to the company and where the outsourcer stabilizes the IT infrastructure by providing a needed role that could not be filled otherwise. This is a more long-term relationship where permanent value needs to be added.

When reviewing what tasks can and cannot be performed internally, an IT manager must be conscious of the impact these decisions will have on the organization and the bottomline. Systems integration and many other outsourced activities can be expensive, but, more importantly, on the cost and impact on the IT environment in the future.

Shopping for an Outsourcer

With all of the possible outcomes from the company's outsourcing decisions, an IT manager should carefully shop for an outsourcing partner. These suggestions can be useful in establishing the parameters for deciding what to outsource in the IT department:

- Estimate the key areas to retain internally, both for core competencies and political expediencies

- Define skill sets within the IT organization and what areas are lacking

- Talk with all user groups in the company to determine what support is needed and for what they are willing to pay

- Define exactly what support level the company requires from an external source

Once an IT manager has defined what areas need to be outsourced, priorities must be set. When a company is new in dealing with outsourcing services, the company should start with a trial portion of the business, as is the case when starting with C/S technology.

When browsing through the outsourcing organization offerings, these guidelines may help a company shop wisely:

- Choose a company whose core business is in the areas of support the company requires. A generalist may not provide the strong levels the company may need.

- The outsourcer should have a proven track record and strategic relationships with computer and software vendors. One sure way to cut through the marketing hype is to ask what technology the company itself uses and supports. If an outsourcer does not run its own software on C/S architecture, how can the company expect it to support its own distributed infrastructure?

- Learn how much and what type of training the outsources provides its own company. After all, if the company is outsourcing because the IT staff cannot expend the time and energy required to keep pace with changing technologies, make sure the company is buying an outsourcer that can.

- Ask for a customer list. Talk with some of the customers or ask to visit a customer's organization. Talk with a customer support person and listen in on a support call.

- Feel comfortable with the outsourcer. An outsourcer must be willing to learn the business's operations and customize its support for the users. Meet with the company's customer support director. The company will be working closely with the firm, so one should feel comfortable with the support team. Ask to have a single account representative dedicated to the company's business.

- Contracts should measure the outsourcer's performance based on benchmarks important to the business. Specify what type of reports are required and how often they need to be submitted.

- Plan to diligently manage the contract. A company may outsource the processes, but not the process ownership. Insert a financial bonus and penalties for meeting establish criteria.

- Performance guarantees are crucial to maintaining control. Plan to review the contract and its performance annually and measure performance against industry standards so the company can reevaluate its service needs, which are likely to change over 10 years.

Managing an Outsourcing Relationship

When the company hires an outsourcer, it is inviting a subcontractor to become an integral part of its business. To receive the most value, the relationship must be efficiently managed.

IT managers are finding outsourcing is similar to a marriage: After the honeymoon is over, hard work keeps the relationship together. Like many newlyweds, the company finds itself, managerially speaking, at the bottom of a steep learning curve.

The pitfalls reside within three broad categories:

1. *Maintaining flexibility in a relationship defined by a not-so-flexible contract.* Too much emphasis on the legal contract between the outsourcer and IT can be an obstacle to achieving success in an outsourcing agreement. If a contract is too rigid in specifying the performance targets, changing circumstances due to new technologies and business goals are bound to make those targets obsolete. The dropping price/performance ratio of hardware, the rising capabilities of packaged software, the emergence of the Internet are all elements that, in recent years, may have made overly rigid performance goals fall short of the targets. This type of rapid change has led to shorter outsourcing contracts, reports Michael F. Corbett, co-founder and research director of the New York City-based Outsourcing Institute, an association of providers and users. In the days of mainframes, contracts were often 10 years or longer; today, three years to five years is more common.

2. *Maintaining control of costs.* The area that causes the most conflicts between outsourcing partners usually deals with money. No matter how friendly everyone appears to be, it is in the outsourcer's interest to encourage clients to spend additional money on IT, not less. The special insider privileges needed to create the effective working relationship can help them target new opportunities. This is not to say that all proposals for expanded outsourcing services are unnecessary, however. A responsible outsourcer is obligated to alert clients to potential problems and offer a solution.

3. *Keeping enough psychological distance to reliably oversee the outsourcer while becoming close enough to effectively work as partners.* The best solutions to problems come from an open environment, where the outsourcing staff is included in planning meetings and encouraged to speak freely.

There is a need to overcome the "us versus them" attitude, because this is the only way to ensure the best technical solutions are aired. However, this close camaraderie can backfire if some constraints are not placed on the outsourcers. When a member of the company expresses a need, perhaps for a faster communications link or better desktop hardware, the outsourcer must understand that no agreement can be consummated without first clearing it with the relationship manager.

The psychological implications of using outsiders to fulfill IT responsibilities should not be discounted either. Many end-users are surprised when they are suddenly dealing with outsiders for support rather than with a member of the internal IT staff. To make matters worse, end-users in general tend to complain more about their IT service when it is being administered by non-corporate personnel, even if the service they receive is the same.

No matter who services the end-users' needs, communications with end-users should be a top priority, not only initially when an outsourcing changeover is in process, but also periodically to give workers a chance to offer feedback about the service. The job of managing the outsourcer can be so consuming to IT staffers that they lose sight of the reasons the outsourcing deal was initially made. Corbett has observed a tendency for IT departments to focus on cost concerns after a while, even though the main reason for outsourcing initially was strategic. For this reason, Jones suggests periodically measuring the progress being made toward attaining specific goals set out in advance;

goals that serve to keep the emphasis on the bigger issues of whether the company's IT function is performing to world-class standards rather than focusing on day-to-day operational issues.

Focusing on these larger goals can be difficult because the members of the IT department are often so involved in the success of the relationship that they have difficulty judging whether they are meeting their outsourcing goals. Further, the growing popularity of outsourcing will lead to a new type of service provider in the next few years – the third-party outsourcing management firm. Such a firm would independently evaluate the effectiveness of the outsourcer in meeting world-class performance targets. There is a tendency for relationship managers and the outsourcer to represent progress reports so the outsourcing appears more profitable than it actually is. Therefore, third-party outsourcing service providers would benefit the top management of a company by providing a non-bias, third-party report. Even then, however, experience shows that IT would probably have to worry about managing the outsourcing manager. Companies assume they can walk away from a project if they turn it over to an outsourcer, stated Jones, but they cannot.

Asset Management

Asset management is critical, and not just for large organizations. The skyrocketing cost of desktop resources has severely affected IT budgets of all sizes. Many organizations underestimate the number of PCs they have by as much as 30% to 35%. Many firms also overestimate the hardware power of those machines. The management thinks the majority of their desktop machines are 486s with 8 MB of RAM, when in fact, says London-based PC audit software vendor fPrint, only about 28% of PCs are at this level in the typical organization. In addition, about one-third are older, 386-based PCs that lack the processing power to support new operating systems such as Windows 95

Being unaware of desktop assets can cost companies money, not necessarily where it is expected. "Beating IBM or Compaq down for a 10% discount may be insignificant over five years," says Gartner Group. "The purchase price is only a piece of the problem, the company should be attacking hidden or soft costs." Hidden costs are estimated to increase the cost as much as 25% over three years, unless the company implements management techniques to bring them under control. Hidden costs include: Time wasted by end-users trying to solve PC problems they are not trained to address; individual departmental spending on software outside the company's IT budget; and over-licensing of networks by organizations buying software for PCs not even in use or which have been "lost."

How does a company manage to track down those assets? These guidelines may help companies see substantial savings:

- *Take inventory*: Maintaining an accurate inventory is an essential element of a good disaster recovery strategy. How can a network get up and running again if no one knows what should be on it?

- *Reevaluate purchasing methods*: Many organizations have not changed their procurement processes since the initial conception of these processes designed for buying mainframes years ago. The PC Asset Management Institute states companies can reduce PC hardware and software expenditures as much as 30% through better procurement management.

- *Discard old equipment*: Few companies anticipate this cost, but after three years, many PCs have a negative residual value, meaning companies will have to pay to dispose of them.

- *License software for only the number of users who need it:* The majority of organizations are over-licensed, say many analysts, some overspending as much as $100,000 a year for needless licenses. Many organizations, for example, have licenses for twice as many Novell NetWare users as they need. Reallocation and license metering can cut these costs.

- *Carefully evaluate the software applications purchased*: Prices for individual programs have dropped, but organizations now buy more of them. A DOS PC ran an average of four or five applications, where a Windows 95 machine usually has 10 or more. Analysts estimate about 5% to 7% of all applications become unused shelfware.

- *Use state-of-the-art software:* Hidden costs can be incurred by continuing to rely on out-of-date software. DOS is the chief culprit. Moving to an OS with a GUI will more than pay for itself because users will quickly adapt to the new environment and require less training and support.

- *Eliminate unauthorized software use*: Some employees, unwilling to wait for applications they want, install applications on their own. These programs can cause problems. In addition to raising licensing issues, they wreak havoc for help desk and support staff, adding expenses to both. They also make it impossible to accurately assess the amount and type of software being used in the organization.

- *Leverage staff expertise*: An analyst at Gartner Group has attributed some off-budget spending to what he calls the "Hey Joe factor." A user with a problem calls a colleague over for help: "Hey Joe, what do you make of this?" Joe does not know, so he gets Larry, and three other people try to solve a problem that is not the job for any of them. A recent KPMG study recently found only 12% of organizations are harnessing the skills of their internal PC "gurus."

- *Outsourcing as a money saver*: Some managers choose outsourcing to reduce costs. Keep in mind the company will be handing over control of major company assets so it is not always the best solution. The IT organization must determine the cost of in-house computing before one can evaluate the potential benefit of outsourcing.

The cost message: IT costs are not in capital outlay or administration. Rather, they are in the systems and software operation over a limited number of years of a life cycle. When companies talk about beating down manufacturers on prices, that is not where the costs really are. For example, LAN costs are in the support and the hidden costs of ownership. Figure 8.2 shows the annual cost of ownership and management expense for PCs in a model based on 5,000 machines in a *Fortune* 1,000.

Figure 8.2 Annual Cost of Desktop Ownership and Management

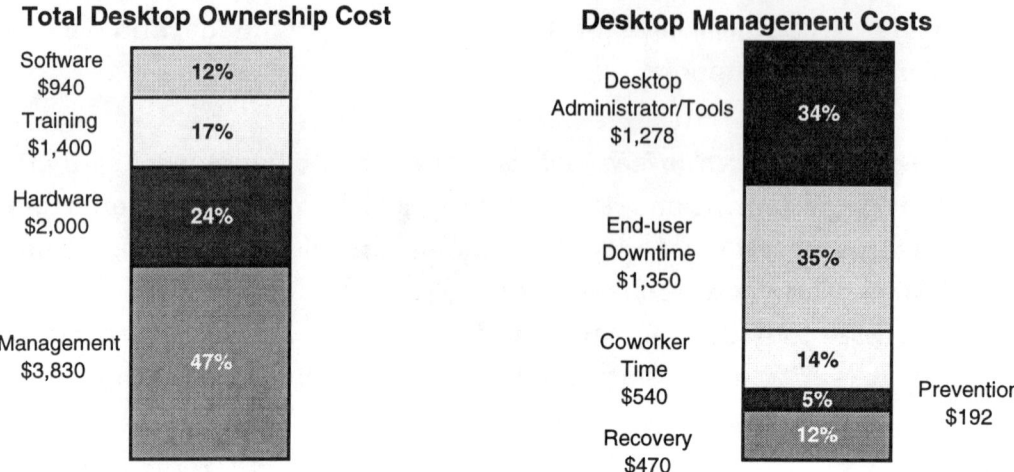

Note: Total desktop ownership cost = $8,170; Desktop management costs = $3,830

Source: Forrester Research, Inc.

IT experts state the first step is for senior management to admit the problem exists and to acknowledge the need for urgent action. However, opinion is divided on where to place the blame of IT asset mismanagement. The blame should be divided between management and the IT industry itself. Industry has been selling next year's solution as the answer to all a company's IT problems. Unless the companies buying these solutions do some work at ground level, the companies will never be able to take advantage of the new solutions.

In the past, senior IT management gave local departmental and unit managers carte blanche to buy what their departments wanted because senior management did not see PCs as strategic to the business. But business strategies are now revolving around these PCs and, whereas management could once control mainframes easily, PCs have grown in use and grown beyond any set boundaries.

The solution, according to the experts, is for corporations to create a database of asset management, calculating the total cost of ownership through evaluating corporate cost in terms of time, staff, money and resources used, and covering every piece of hardware and software. The ideal enterprise asset management combines business and technology tactics to keep a fiscal and physical track of a company's IT assets.

Otherwise, a company can fall into the passive IT management trap. According to London-based PC audit software vendor fPrint: "We audit eight large companies with 500-plus PCs every month and we find only 28% of PCs meet the IT directors' current specifications, and these are in corporations which are talking about rolling out Windows 95 in the next three months. We have also found 27% of PCs are not networked and 38% of networked PCs are not accessible from one central point. It is common in these organizations to find four or five different network environments in the same building, which is an enormous waste and something that must be addressed by management."

Companies must track their IT assets from start to finish, asking questions such as: "How did each piece of hardware and software get here?" "Who uses it?" "Is it changing?" "Who is having problems with it and what is its salvage value?" Knowing what they have and how they can use it can dramatically lower the total cost of IT in the organization. The tools are now available to provide a solution to this dilemma, and organizations should approach the challenge as soon as feasible.

Reduction as an Interoperable Option

In this case, as a function of asset management, reduction is defined as limiting the number of systems and software the company supports. Reduction can be called "downsizing," "rightsizing" or a number of other names, but the main question is: Can it save the company money to reduce the number of different environments the company currently maintains? This issue goes beyond even downsizing to the desktop level. If the company has multiple desktop environments (for example: Mac and different processors of PCs; 286 through Pentium, plus Windows 3.1, Windows 95, Windows NT, DOS-based applications, etc.), the amount of effort to keep users updated to the right application release is very time consuming.

The recent trends from central mainframe computing to C/S and distributed computing to "save money" have not all been proven to be cost-effective moves. Changing the IT strategy to favor one desktop OS, one flavor of

UNIX, one type of network, etc. may reduce the long-term cost of ownership for the company's IT bill. However, the short-term moving process can be costly if the company is heavily invested in legacy code and systems or has acquired a number of subsidiaries with different IT structures, operating platforms and/or applications.

The most common cost advantage of moving from mainframes to C/S comes from buying off-the-shelf applications versus writing and maintaining the company's own program code. As a result, companies that have successfully migrated from mainframes to C/S offer consistent advice: Whenever possible, buy rather than build. Figure 8.3 shows a 1993 study by Forrester Research on the allocation of total costs under a C/S environment. Application development is 28% of the total cost allocation, in comparison, according to Forrester, to an AS/400 environment which is 40% for application development.

Figure 8.3 Allocation of Total Costs for Client/Server

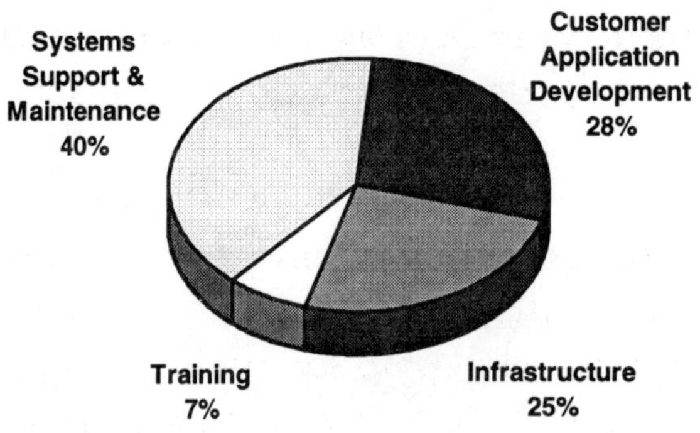

Source: Forrester Research, Inc.

For example, as a result of moving from mainframes to C/S, Motorola's General Systems Sector (GSS) in Schaumberg, Illinois reduced total computing costs from 3.2% of annual revenue in 1989, to 0.8% in 1994, for a total reduction of almost 50%. From 1989 to 1991, that translated into $150 million in savings. As part of its C/S transition, Motorola purchased more than 75% of its software, including all of its financial applications and almost all of its order-entry and materials requirement planning (MRP) packages. For a few strategic manufacturing applications, GSS continued to develop its own code. For those applications, the company discarded COBOL and used tools such as Informix 4GLs, Oracle Forms, and JYACC's Java Animation Machine (JAM) for screen generators. The GSS division manufactures cellular infrastructure equipment and UNIX and Windows NT systems.

At Motorola, total computing costs include equipment and labor for the IT department, non-IT departments, and data communications. In the general-manufacturing sector of the U.S. economy, IT budgets have accounted for 40% to 70% of total computing costs.

According to industry figures, software expenditures for a 4,300-class mainframe can easily approach $30,000 per month, including coding from the ground-up, maintaining and modifying software, and purchasing applications.

Motorola GSS has jettisoned all of its mainframes. However, most companies have only begun to back-off from the mainframe and solidify their migration plans. These companies offer the following advice: Monitor and learn from peers and competitors. For example, Texas Instruments began its transition strategy by consulting and sharing cost-analysis data with more than a dozen companies in the manufacturing sector.

Like Motorola, Texas Instruments expected the bulk of its cost savings to come from buying off-the-shelf applications. Traditionally, mainframe-centric Texas Instruments has written virtually all of its application code. As part of its C/S transition strategy, The company planned to purchase all of its non-competitive applications, including IT-run human resources and accounting packages.

From making the buy-versus-build decision, Texas Instruments expected to cut computing costs from 4% to 5% of annual revenue to less than 3% during the course of its planned three- to four-year transition. Approximately 90% of Texas Instrument's IT computing operations are currently hosted by IBM mainframes. As a result of the transition from the programmer-intensive mainframes, rather than reduce its headcount, Texas Instruments planned to redeploy programming personnel into its competitive applications such as semiconductor manufacturing.

Although Texas Instruments expects to see a 30% decrease in computing costs as a result of the transition to C/S, cost savings are just one benefit. The main reason for migrating, according to their IT manager, is to accelerate business process changes to gain competitive advantages. Measuring computing costs as a percentage of annual revenue is only one way to benchmark the potential financial advantages of moving to C/S.

Another metric to watch is revenue per IT employee. More of the costs associated with maintaining mainframes come from people and labor costs than from hardware and software and maintenance costs.

As a result of its downsizing effort, Sun Microsystems, Inc. was able to increase its revenue per IT employee from $1.9 million in 1989, to $4.8 million in 1994. By the fiscal year end of 1995, that figure had grown to $5.5 million.

According to Terry Keeley, vice president and chief architect in the Sun Information Resources division in Mountain View, California, although Sun was able to reduce computing costs by 60%, little of the savings is attributable to the buy versus build decision. In fact, buying applications ranked a distant fourth among the factors affecting cost savings.

Keeley attributes cost reductions first to Sun's migration of decision support systems off the mainframe onto C/S systems, which eliminated centralized report generation and distribution.

A shift to automated software distribution and license management was the second biggest cost reducer. Sun uses its own SunDANS package for software distribution, version control, tracking software use, and license control across a WAN with more than 17,000 UNIX workstations, 4,000 servers, 1,500 PCs, and one remaining mainframe, which is used for manufacturing, distribution, and some order management functions.

The third biggest cost reduction contributor at Sun was the decision to use dataless workstations, which include disk drives but no permanent data storage. All applications are managed at the server level. Dataless workstations are the only appropriate way to implement C/S while reducing costs, contends Keeley.

When it came to the buy-versus-build decision, Sun did not opt to buy everything. It did buy all of its TP applications, but built virtually all of its decision support systems. Sun justified the cost of dedicating programmers to decision support systems because transaction systems have a useful life of roughly five to seven years, and decision support systems have a useful life of only six months to two years, added Keeley.

Although many companies that have migrated to C/S emphasize the cost savings from reduced software development time, Sun downplays development costs. IT infrastructure costs eclipse development budgets by three to four times. At Sun, infrastructure costs ran 75% to 80% of the IT budget before its migration to C/S; after the migration, Sun reduced that figure to 42%.

Most companies that have downsized from mainframes do not attribute significant cost savings to a reduction in personnel, although much fewer people are required to maintain computing and network operations. According to research examining nine companies, including Texas Instruments, Motorola, and Sun, conducted by Ernst & Young's Center for Business Innovation in Boston, the companies spent on average 4.6% of total business revenue on computing in 1993. By 1994, that figure had dropped to only 4.4%. The study surveyed two telecommunications companies and seven high-tech manufacturing companies that were in various stages of migrating from mainframes to C/S.

Charles Gold, a researcher at Ernst & Young, says many companies attribute all of their cost savings to the shift to C/S when, in fact, some of those savings came from activities that had little or nothing to do with C/S architectures. Examples include decreasing mainframe prices, hardware depreciation factors, and the consolidation of dataprocessing centers.

In addition, moving to C/S shifts computing work (labor costs) from IT to end-users. In essence, some cost savings with C/S are essentially cost transfers that the company has not been able to track previously.

Customization at What Cost?

One approach to IT management calls for companies to leave overall network management and administration to in-house IT staffs, while contracting with

---

outside programmers for development of specialized applications. In-house IT staffs are under increasing pressure to perform a variety of functions. Often, such staffs lack the time and personnel required to develop or modify legacy departmental applications. One way to avoid this problem would be to make in-house IT personnel responsible for specifying a standard set of development tools and acceptable outside programmers. Particular departments could then contract with these outside professionals to develop and install custom applications. The in-house staff could consult on such projects as necessary, but would mainly be involved in the day-to-day operation of the enterprise network. Many find this interesting, but have not yet accepted this particular IT management mindset in their organization.

The shift to object-based application modules presents opportunities for custom software, but all companies need extensive training to capitalize on the trend. Objects allow software applications to be built to customer specifications, but constructing the applications will be difficult. ParaTechnology, Inc. President Peter Raulerson says 43% of IT customers hire outside integrators for a skills transfer; integrators and resellers who learn to build custom applications from object libraries will be best positioned through the mid-1990s. Gartner Group, Inc. senior vice president Michael Braude says testing applications is time consuming, and it can be just as time consuming to test applications built from objects; value-added resellers (VARs) must become systems integrators.

At what cost does software customization by VARs or others affect the IT business internally? A trend in IT is the role of software as a source of competitive advantage. A company might decide it wants a certain application, and simply hire a firm to write it. The customization cost includes the expense to write and maintain, but its value is protected by treating it as a trade secret, because it is worth more to the company as a uniquely functioning component rather than as a tradeable asset. The reuse of the software or knowledge by the custom software supplier would be governed by a specific contract with the underlying assumption the actual code and some of the features and functions are protected by copyright.

Many services are best done in-house, but companies such as ADP and First Data Resources have made huge and profitable businesses handling payroll, insurance adjustments, and financial transactions as outsourced services. The cost to the company using the outsourcing services is both a control cost and a service cost, but the savings comes from taking advantage of the expertise in these areas, which comes from the volume of work done by these organizations.

One increasingly popular customization method involves companies pooling resources to fund the development of software they need. For example, CommerceNet, a not-for-profit consortium of companies that want to do commerce over the Internet, has contracted with Enterprise Integration Technologies (EIT) to develop much of the software infrastructure its members will use. (Much of that infrastructure is based on free software that is being connected by EIT.)

Consider the example of PRT Corp.'s project for Merck. The pharmaceutical giant originally hired PRT, a systems integrator, to develop an add-on data conversion and testing tools for the high-end human resources package it had licensed from Tesseract. To cover the costs, Merck encouraged PRT to market the same code to Chevron and Bristol-Myers. PRT and Merck shared the license fees from those two customers; PRT had promised to provide Merck with free maintenance and upgrades, based on its ability to sell them to the other customers. The result: Tesseract reacted by offering an equivalent capability for free. Now the three companies are using PRT's software, and PRT supports it, for a fee, as necessary, but PRT is doing no more development on it.

Another example of group efforts is the internal service that becomes a commercial resource. For example, the airline reservation systems originally developed by a single airline and are now offered, at high profitability, to other airlines (partly due to customer demand for consolidated data). American Airlines' Sabre system is the premier example, still owned by American, but sold as a service to other airlines and thousands of travel agents. By contrast, Galileo International's Galileo product is now owned by a consortium of airlines.

There are many approaches to covering the customization costs, but a key point to remember is the long-term costs and benefits. The long-term cost of maintaining the code in terms of knowledge and programmers should be outweighed by the competitive advantage the customized software provides.

Interoperability of Personnel

The IT profession is changing as business skills become more important than technical expertise. The traditional barriers between IT and end-users have never been successful and the future will require open system development, with developers and end-users working together. There are several stages involved in any major change: Shock, defensive retreat, acceptance, adaptation, and growth. The IT profession has many examples of shock and defensive retreat, it is now time for professionals to accept the reality and to adapt. One adaptation problem has been a breakdown in communication between end-users and both internal IT departments and external suppliers. High staff turnover, redundancy, and outsourcing have disrupted relationships, and this is being felt in impaired information flows.

The training issue of IT staff in these days of outsourcing and decentralization is a concern. Employers often hire outside consultants to do work employees believes they could do if they had the training. Problems in personnel occur for those who want to keep pace with current technology, but are reduced to using mainframe development skills due to lack of exposure to new technologies.

The fact that management would rather hire contractors than train its own people is demoralizing to the staff in many cases. This demoralization can be an attributed fact to high staff turnover. IT management looks for the short-term, higher cost solution of outsourcing than the longer-term, ultimately lower cost of training and education.

As a result, IT departments face complex management issues caused by the drastically short supply of experienced IT personnel with C/S skills, while C/S experts bounce from job to job and command large salaries. The shortage of experienced personnel is so severe many companies have lost personnel at an alarming rate. Consultancies have drawn personnel from company IT departments with lavish salaries, justifying the costs by charging desperate IT departments enormous prices for their services. A recent survey of human resources executives by staffing services provider Olsten Corp. of Melville, New York found 52% of IT departments are understaffed. In the United States, the starting salary for a beginning C/S software developer on the east coast is twice as high as experienced COBOL programmers. Some companies have tried stemming the losses by approving large salary increases and offering bonuses designed to promote employee retention, but company loyalty is a rarity in the C/S market.

How does a company maintain its staff and make them a part of the business advantage IT can provide the company?

- *Paying technology bonuses*: This is an obvious tactical approach to attracting and retaining critical IT skills. IT managers considering this approach should be cautious, however. Technology bonuses can create more management problems than they solve. For one thing, they can cause resentment from employees not offered bonuses. Structuring such packages can be difficult. Managers are forced to predict in advance how long a company will be willing to pay a premium for a specific skill.

- *Accentuate the positive aspects of an in-house job:* While a high-paying consulting job might initially seem alluring to a C++ programmer, thoroughly explain the job description; a consulting job generally means almost constant travel. And the employer will probably want the new consultant to concentrate on one specific skill for an extended period of time. An IT organization, on the other hand, can offer perks such as continuity, regular hours, and the chance to learn new skills.

- *Take a long-term approach to skills assessment and management:* Make skills development an integral part of business and IT planning. Managers are asked to predict, given business and technology direction, what their skills requirements will be. Then, an analysis is done to identify the gaps between current and future skill levels and needs. Training programs are created to develop the skills and competencies that will be needed.

Skills assessment and management, also known as skills-based management, is catching on at many IT organizations. The idea: Instead of scrambling to assemble hard-to-find skills on a reactive, project-by-project basis, organizations can create long-term strategies for developing and retaining needed IT skills. The technique involves first creating detailed job descriptions and then determining associated skills or attributes. Xerox Corp., an early proponent of skills-based management for IT, has identified a pool of 119 skills and attributes needed by its IT organization. Some of which include business skills, technical skills, and leadership skills. Managers assess the organization's current inventory of skills, identifying gaps and training courses that individuals can take to gain needed skills.

Proponents say skills-based management has a couple of advantages. First, it can help managers anticipate and plan for changing skill requirements in their organizations. Second, it can provide individual employees a clear picture of how they can increase their value to the organization by gaining needed new skills.

IT personnel whose jobs change to emphasize working with end-users rather than other IT employees will have to develop skills that facilitate career advancement. Working with end-users will give IT personnel a thorough understanding of the company's issues and help users accept new technology and systems. On the other hand, IT personnel working in the end-user environment will strengthen their negotiation and communication skills. However, it is wise to maintain contact with former IT peers to prevent interpersonal conflicts from arising. Maintaining contact with new management is vital to prevent being victimized by the "out of sight, out of mind" syndrome during raise or promotion opportunities. Lastly, IT personnel should realize it takes time to develop quality relationships with new co-workers.

There is a new trend among ex-mainframe personnel: A rising demand among IT departments for older ex-mainframe sales and support staff and also for those with account management experience in facilities management. User companies are taking them on as relationship managers, not necessarily full-time. This points out how the skills of maintaining technology for end-users does not necessarily change with the technology itself. This also stresses that a dual skill set is needed to be successful in IT today: Technical expertise and business relationship acumen.

Chapter 9

Future Trends

With all of the dynamic changes in today's IT environment, what does the future hold for the interoperable IT operation? The proverbial crystal ball is a bit fuzzy, but there are a few certainties that can be predicted. First, as the computing model continues to change, the Internet will play a significant role in the future IT infrastructure, both on a home and on a business level. Second, end-users will take a commodity view of computing as standards on the desktop improve ease-of-use and ease-of-interaction. Of course, the role that IT will continue to play as a competitive advantage to the business' bottomline.

The Internet as Part of the Solution

The current role of IT in society is moving toward what HP calls "persuasive IS," in which the Internet is the backbone of an IT infrastructure to provide the level of service everyone expects. Figure 9.1 is a continuum first shown in 1983 at an HP briefing. Notice how consistent it is toward today's environment.

Figure 9.1 Toward Persuasive Information Systems

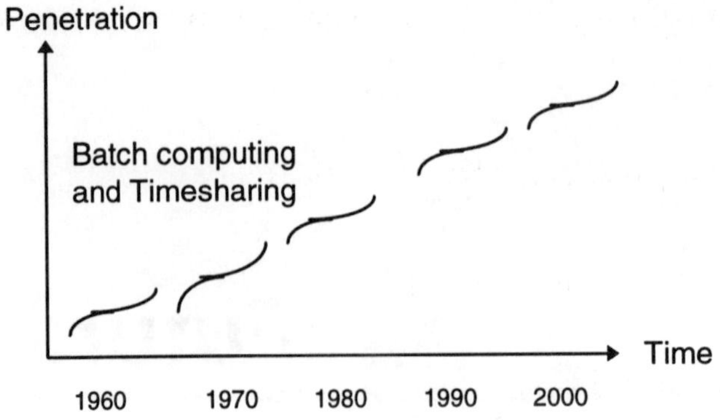

Source: Hewlett-Packard

IT departments must bring to computing what the Internet and the Web have brought to data. The Internet has created a standard format (HTML), a semi-standard front-end (Web browsers), and a standard method of data and information transference. Many organizations want to make internal use of Web browsers, which serve as universal clients and allow users to access information and interact with Web servers in a graphical way regardless of the system used. However, as the Web evolves, it is becoming more complex in its applications and usage.

The introduction of complexity, in turn, makes interoperability more difficult. The Web today is truly open. Web servers and Web browsers are interoperable because the protocols are simple and uniformly implemented. Now that the Web has evolved from a research project where concepts such as profit and market share were non-issues to a burgeoning market-driven industry, the industry is beginning to see proprietary extensions to HTML so a particular vendor's Web server product works best with that vendor's browser. This may have the negative effect of requiring users to implement multiple browsers, perhaps using browser A because it works best with the user's stock quoting service, and browser B because it is optimized to work with the user's local department store server. The complexity will increase further until the inevitable "standards" wars are waged and resolved.

The role of IT in the business environment has been significantly assisted by the Internet boom. The challenge, now that the infrastructure questions are less prevalent, is the management of the information provided because more information access is available. Computing is becoming more a service than a product, and the environment it works in is becoming more service-oriented. In that respect, computing turns from a captive investment into a competitive service.

Requirements of computing in the future will still include:

- Distributed process ownership

- Enterprise capabilities

- Universal information access

- Robust communications

Computing as a service should answer these requirements: It would provide a transparent, scalable, and heterogeneous environment which would be secure, reliable, and manageable in terms of computing resources. Using the model of a Web browser and Internet network infrastructure, future computing would have heterogeneous clients and decentralized servers, resulting in a lesser financial investment with incremental additions. In terms of investment, this model would use volume technologies as the "appliances" for the front-end, while using high-performance and legacy systems as the power drivers in the "back office." The security aspects would be built-in to the OS and into the network.

The processing power issue, as shown in Figure 9.2, is in parallel with the issue of interconnectivity. As one moves up the enterprise and includes business partners and customers (the "extended enterprise") in its realm, the processing power issue increases proportionally. This is another area where the Internet capabilities are infrastructurally necessary.

Figure 9.2 Trends in Processing Power

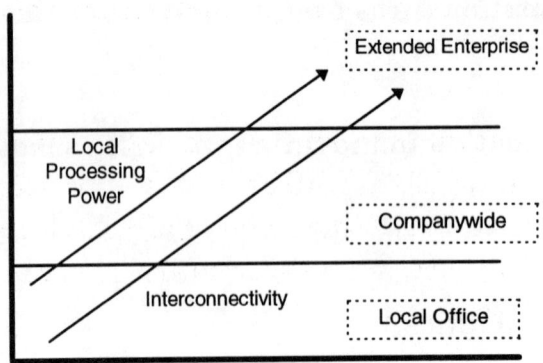

This model would be manageable because the necessary IT resources would be mainly hardware (as a commodity), LANs, and applications, which could be ultimately downloaded as an applet from the Web. The infrastructure, front-end, and security are provided by the general Internet structure and the OS and operating structure of the environment.

Figure 9.3 IT Pyramid

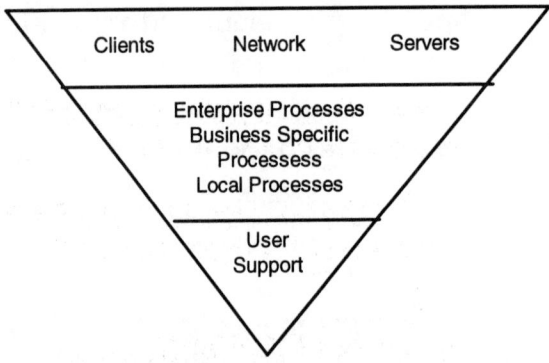

Within the IT Pyramid (see Figure 9.3) the client and network portion of the figure can be assumed by the Web model, and the user support and desktop management can be assumed by desktop standards, outsouring, and Web browsers in the future. The value proposition of IT in the future will, therefore, be in the management of the application processes, no matter where the process is taking place or how they add to business efficiency and effectiveness. Software vendors such as CA, Boole and Babbage, Candle, and others are spending effort providing business process management tools for this reason. According to Meta Group, however, distributed C/S application management products are still three to five years in the future, with business process management products more than seven to 10 years away.

For control of the infrastructure and its costs, the Internet's performance is key to its continued growth, but will require a concerted effort by ISPs and corporate Internet users to resolve a number of critical issues. While security, viruses, and reliability are primary concerns, issues such as employee productivity are also significant.

Security is the most critical issue for corporate users and is usually managed with the installation of fire walls. However, information sent to and from the server remains insecure. With the virtual corporation (partners and customers included within the enterprise environment), security features such as tunneling, the ability to create a secure link between firewalls, has been a necessary step for the evolution of the intranet solution, shown in Figure 9.4.

Figure 9.4 Evolution of Internet Use

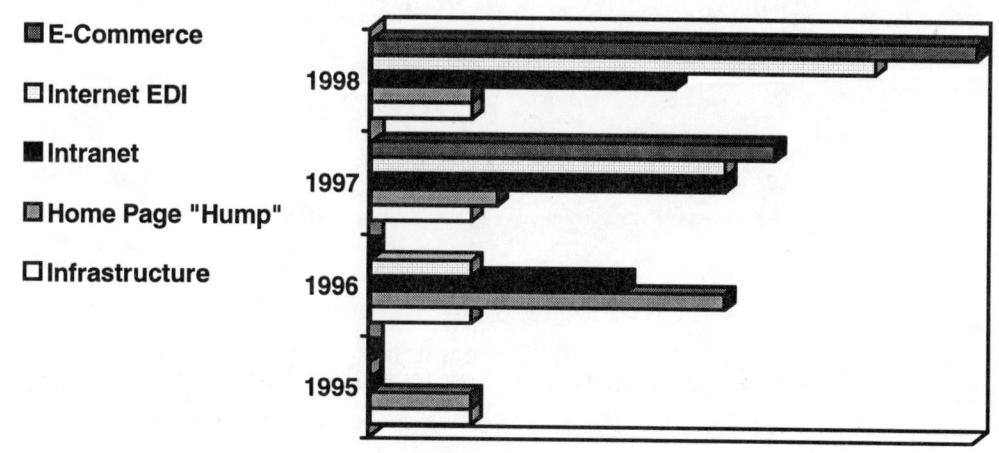

Source: Hewlett-Packard

TCP/IP ensures the reliable, eventual transfer of information, but it is impeded by Internet traffic blockages. Several ISPs have addressed congestion by adding FR backbones to their networks. Scalability is another concern because the ability to send voice and video over the Internet will increase bandwidth requirements. TCP/IP and scalability are two more reasons for the implementation of technologies such as ISDN and ATM in communications.

Barriers to the Intranet Solutions

There are two major barriers to the success of the Internet and intranet as part of the enterprise IT solution: Technological and managerial issues. From a technological standpoint, one could argue the major inhibitors are bandwidth and scalability, both in networks and in software. With any "new" technology, demand outpaces improvement, and when improvement in the technology comes, capacity improves by an order of magnitude. Therefore, the technological demands are always a step behind the actual capability, which will continue throughout the evolution of technology.

Today's main Internet and intranet technical challenges can be summarized as:

- *Content:* Two aspects of content are of current concern.

    1. Providing the most effective enterprise data in the right format or interface for the user or browser.

    2. Internally connecting all the correct aspects to create the appropriate data structure for "data mining" or correlation of different data sources to create the "aha" effect.

- *Scalability:* In essence, the need for middleware within the Internet environment, similar to what has occurred with TP monitors and with relational databases. When using the Internet, the user places a request with the browser, the browser sends a message to the Web server, the Web server returns a page or two of data, then disconnects. There is no interactive relationship, and the Web browser will become a bottleneck over time in this type of request scenario.

- *Strength:* Because Web servers are still in their infancy, they lack the time-worn strength of enterprise servers and their components, such as administrative, security, and utility tools.

- *Flexibility:* As with any new technology area, no particular supplier can address all the needs of an IT organization. For now, companies will have to rely on more than one vendor to solve its technological requirements.

- *Application Development:* The key to Internet growth are applications using the infrastructure – electronic commerce, supply chain integration, securities industry trading, etc. These types of applications require secure development and certain equipment add-ons (such as credit card "swiping" machines) to integrate into the IT environment.

To overcome the technical challenges of the 'Net, companies should assess the new solutions possible and how their own technical solutions currently correspond to meeting the new solution needs.

According to a recent study by The Aberdeen Group of Boston, the areas of equipment and services of the most concern are:

- *Server hardware:* The needs of a Web server and of enterprise servers are different, based on usage and services provided. A Web server must handle both text-database requests and communications requests, therefore, these servers must be optimized for the type of small query, large response transactions end-users will require. This includes servers that are multithreading and load balancing with rapid communications abilities.

- *RDBMS:* With the advent of sophisticated graphics requests on the Internet, databases must handle more object-oriented technology, and varied data and text requests. Therefore, a RDBMS that extends its capabilities with object-relational technology support will be a longer-term solution.

- *Middleware:* Scaling Internet and intranet architectures requires typical TP monitor-like functions such as server-side load balancing. To assemble the pieces, middleware is the key element of the Internet picture.

- *Tools and administrative software:* With intranets, administration can, in effect, cross company boundaries. The increased difficulty accessing all data needed by enterprise end-users involves a more complex corporate directory service/data dictionary than currently used. Corporate directory services is an area where building a data repository would be useful.

- *Networking infrastructure:* The Internet is the external backbone, but remember the internal one: The network will be required to scale in terms of usage of the Internet.

- *C/S set-up:* In general, a review of the applications and tools, including data "mining" tools, must occur to see how they can incorporate the Internet technology and their usefulness with intranets.

The real barrier to Internet and intranet solutions is management, the organizational culture, and its psychological approach to the use of technology.

A number of analogies can be used to visualize the view of non-IT management to the Internet culture. First, one of the selling points of the Internet for a corporate environment is the seamless access to information throughout the company. Non-IT management can view this capability as a "step backward" because it is an immature paradigm replacing a mature paradigm. Once the regulatory environment evolves in the next two years, however, this will be viewed more as a mature paradigm and viewed as a business advantage.

In terms of business advantage, the Internet can be paralleled with the advent of toll-free telephone numbers. Initially, companies implementing toll-free telephone numbers only saw the cost and long-term investment. For example, they had to train telephone support forces, pay additional telephone costs, and manage the additional feedback and problems that occurred. Once companies realized the potential of the medium, however, it became a business advantage to provide customers cost-free telephone access to the company. In 1995, the number of toll-free "minutes" was greater than the number of typical minutes logged for the first time in the United States. Again, once corporations realize the electronic advantage to customers and potential customers having cost-free access to the company, they will start taking advantage of the business opportunities provided.

As with any new concept, there are early adopters and mainstream adopters. Usually, the early adopters work out the "bugs" for the rest. This is what is currently happening with security issues such as firewalls, tunneling, Web browser standards, and HTML standards. Similar to the advent of credit cards and even telemarketing, any new way of transmitting personal information in a non-personal way makes people nervous.

On an enterprise level, the intranet can be paralleled with the advent of groupware. Both involve sharing enterprise data and information with others in the organization and both involve a new way of working. Groupware and the intranet are both collaborative technologies that affect the way people intercommunicate. The impact on communications affects the way people work and eventually the structure of the organization. The difficulty most organizations encounter with groupware is not with the technology, but with the relationship between technology and the people in the organization who use groupware.

The Internet technology such as groupware requires change and change management. Change management is a group of practices and technologies that evolved out of the field of organizational development and management consulting. Planning for change drastically improves the chance of success. Additionally, organizations tend to resist change in proportion to their size. The larger the organization, the greater the resistance (to an exponential degree). In addition, the bigger the change, the greater the resistance. The Web challenge: These technologies have an affect on the way people work and communicate, which magnifies the degree of change and can engender strong opinions either for or against the technology.

As in any other cutting-edge technology, the way to overcome non-user fears of change is to demonstrate its possibilities and potential by usage. As organizational hierarchies flatten, competitive cultures will become collaborative, and business processes will become more efficient and information-driven with the help of the company's intranet.

Desktop Standards and Commonalties: The DMTF

The majority of business computer end-users are on a desktop platform, with more than 170 million PCs installed globally. By the late 1990s, 100 million PC units are expected to ship worldwide each year – more shipments than cars, radios, and TVs.

Few of these computing resources remain standalone. Information is worthless unless connected and shared, and the explosion in the network growth, including online information networks, home users, small offices, and remote connectivity by mobile PC users, highlights the need for connectivity. Networks, growing at the rate of 10 million new PCs a year, are an indispensable aspect of doing business in the 1990s.

The PC has historically been unmanageable and needed expert intervention for the user to fully understand and control. Users of tomorrow's PCs will demand PCs that work as manageable, cohesive units, systems that can self-configure, self-adjust, and communicate with the user. Building the enabling technology for smart, managed PCs and deploying it across the vendor community is the mission and goal of the DMTF.

The DMTF is an industry-wide consortium committed to making PCs easier to use, understand, configure, and manage. The DMTF's goal is to provide the PC platform with a flexible management paradigm and the ingredient technology to meet the information demands of the current and future computing environment.

During the past few years, the DMTF has made significant progress toward their objectives. Transcending traditional competitiveness among PC industry participants, the DMTF has remained on course with its vision of a new generation of manageable PCs. The DMTF's accomplishments represent the work of more than 350 hardware and software vendors, including leading companies in the PC industry.

In October 1993, less than two years after its founding, the DMTF delivered a developers' release of the desktop management interface (DMI). The DMI was the industry's first OS-independent and protocol-independent API for managing the PC.

By July 1994, the industry's first standard Management Information Format (MIF) was delivered by the DMTF's PC Systems Working Committee, the first step in determining what defines a PC system, how it can identify itself to management software, and how it can become a self-managing system for every user to understand and use.

Developing to the DMI offers suppliers an opportunity to differentiate and add value to their products. The DMI allows them to emphasize both standard and vendor-specific features in their products and supports existing standards such as SNMP and Plug and Play.

Standards such as Plug and Play are one aspect of automating and simplifying how PCs are used, focusing on the physical attributes of components, primarily add-in cards and the installation and configuration of hardware. Plug and play addresses these issues on PC platforms under the Windows environment.

Plug and play is in line with the DMTF's efforts to make desktop computing less complex and more manageable for both LAN administrators and PC users alike. The DMI supports Plug and Play by mapping information into the standard PC systems MIF as defined by the PC Systems Working Committee.

The DMI allows manageability by enabling DMI-calling applications to access MIF information, providing the chance for the development of new kinds of powerful management software. The DMI is independent of OS and processor, enabling the development of manageable PC products and applications across platforms.

Currently, desktop management of software is as complex under Windows 95 as it is with Windows 3.1. Managing desktop hardware and software resources is draining many IT organizations. In fact, the Gartner Group estimates IT departments spend up to 80% of the lifetime costs of PCs on their management and only 20% initially purchasing PC hardware and software. The promising view: Standards such as DMI and SNMP and some of the built-in management features of Windows 95 will assist to unlocking the management gridlock.

Utilizing the DMI will initially have concrete benefits at the enterprise level but ultimately across all computing environments, including the home and small office, home "edutainment," and mobile use. For example, a user may want to connect to a workstation via modem, but does not know the modem's communication parameters. A modem using the DMI would report all of its current communication parameters to the MIF database. Rather than going to the modem, the user would access this information from the desktop by querying the MIF database stored on the network. The user discovers the modem is running at 9,600 baud with eight data, even parity, and zero stop bit, which allows a connection to begin.

DMI-enabled PC products will evolve into an improved model of PC understanding and support, a model which gives users the ability to discover what is happening inside the PC and control it. This new relationship between user and PC will be essential for growth as computing and communications spiral into a single tool for users.

Consider information on DMI with a warning. While the DMI is backed by many leading industry vendors who believe the initiative will help users integrate management tools more easily, the standard is still immature, and there have been some disputes between PC vendors about how it should be implemented. Few installed PCs are DMI-enabled. Although PC vendors, including AST, Dell, DEC, HP, and IBM, are selling the marketing hype, analysts predict that less than 10% of all PCs were DMI-enabled by the end of 1995. "DMI will be relevant in the long term, but it is not something an IT manager must be concerned about today," said Andrew Watson, director of desktop marketing at Compaq and a DMTF steering committee member in a recent press article.

For now, most users will have to assemble solutions for themselves. One option for large network administrators is to leverage existing SNMP-based network management platforms such as OpenView or NetView. Windows 95 includes a SNMP agent, MIB, and support for TCP/IP and IPX, but its use is recommended only until desktop management interface becomes widespread because SNMP is limited in its system management functionality.

Continuing Role of IT in Company Business Objectives

There is still a viable role for IT to play in the changing nature of information access. In Figure 9.5, the IT infrastructure is shown as the basis for business innovation and information sharing. In the integration of the enterprise, the challenge is information management. This challenge is focused on learning and knowledge because the input/output (I/O) channel of human beings has not changed with the acceleration of technology. Information is important because it is the basis of decision making, including the decision on company goals and objectives.

Figure 9.5 Information Technology Roles

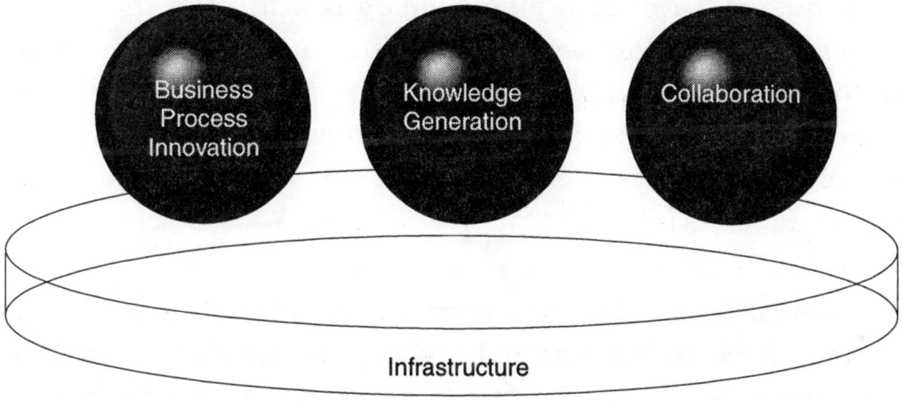

Source: Hewlett-Packard

Over time, business is developing a clearer picture of the relationship between IT and productivity. However, productivity measurement is not an exact science. Although it is understandable managers want clear-cut figures, far more research and calculations must be done before the last word is written on IT effectiveness. The realities of using IT to create customer value can also be intangible in nature.

Perhaps the most important issue: No matter what the figures say about the "average" return on IT investment, IT managers must still decide which projects are worthwhile. There is no financial institution where companies can deposit IT investments and withdraw an "average" return.

The opposite is true, however, because some financial institutions were quietly harvesting returns in the hundred of millions of dollars on their IT investments at the height of the discontent with computer productivity. Productivity does not automatically follow IT dollars, but takes hard work and strategic thinking.

Even when high productivity is achieved, it does not automatically translate into competitive advantage. In fact, a single-minded focus on productivity can be counter productive. Providing a competitive advantage comes from delivering what customers value and from doing so in a unique way that cannot be easily duplicated.

Because productivity and effectiveness are usually looked upon to involve an emphasis on reducing costs and increasing throughput, it detracts from areas such as customer service, quality, and timeliness. These areas are not always measurable, but they are often places where IT can have the bigger impact. Customer values have shifted from mass consumption toward subtler, quality-of-life issues. Although conventional measures of productivity are better at accounting for physical I/O, there is no reason to rely solely on these factors.

During the last few years, many companies have tried to connect IT investment to business strategy. Nearly all organizations have found it difficult, when challenged, to formally place a value on what type of return they receive on the money they invest in IT. All too often, the connections are attempted through special exercises led by IT management or they are discouraged because a technology fanatic drives through an expense unrelated to business direction.

By contrast, the most successful approach is where there are no IT strategies, only business strategies. Here, the IT department adds value by building informed relationships with key business units, ensuring IT requirements become an integral component of business strategy (see Figure 9.6).

Figure 9.6 Vision of IT's Role in the Enterprise

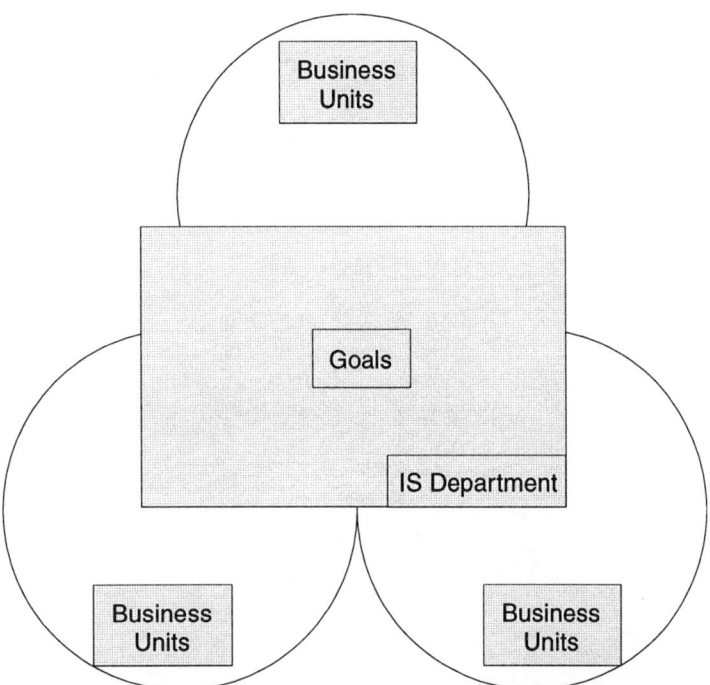

The typical approach of basing an investment decision on whether a new technology increases productivity may sound sensible, but it misses an important point. Technology is only a tool, and one rivals can acquire. If a company tries to focus its competitive advantage on technology alone, it will soon find itself imitated. Technology must be aligned with the core competencies of the company to deliver true value.

Chapter 10

Conclusion

The road to achieving interoperability can be fraught with pitfalls. Interoperable, open systems do not simply plug-in to existing networks and automatically create an environment in-line with an enterprise's business objectives. Even with all of the network and systems management tools available, today an enterprise must still align its systems and networks together with its business model and implement a strategy for long-term deployment with its users needs in mind.

Interoperability is both an approach and a methodology an enterprise may follow to plan, design, and implement standards-based, user-friendly solutions. Using this approach, an enterprise can create an environment that supports its business objectives in the long term. Organizing IT as a tool to be used with other tools to achieve business goals is a realistic view of how an enterprise can gain the competitive advantage. Technology, with its products and services, is a tool that can both add to and detract from what the business is trying to accomplish. Interoperability is a means to connect the technology pieces of the puzzle to help management find more creative solutions. Interoperability brings a method of sharing and creating value from the information resources available to the enterprise.

By concentrating its efforts on using IT in its business processes, the enterprise can best harness the information and knowledge by circulating it through the company. Knowledge management is a popular area in business today. Because of downsizing, frequent job jumping, constant change, globalization, and the shift from an industrial to a knowledge-based economy, companies feel more pressure than ever to maintain an information edge. Therefore, increasing productivity and gaining competitive advantage has become a key issue for many companies. By creating an interoperable organization, knowledge can be shared as a resource and harnessed even after the employee who created the knowledge leaves the company. Information is a company asset, although sometimes intangible, and needs to be encapsulated using IT.

In summary, interoperability benefits the enterprise by improving productivity, increasing efficiency, adding flexibility to the environment, and enhancing the investment made in diverse systems and networks. Interoperability can be implemented most effectively by combining technological standards and commonalties, blended within flexible, business-oriented IT organizations.

Glossary

Application Programming Interface (API) A set of rules describing how to write applications that will interact with other applications or operating systems.

Asynchronous Transfer Mode (ATM) A communications industry standard defined for use in wide area networks (WANs) to support digital transmissions of all types, including data, voice, and video.

Cellular Digital Packet Data (CDPD) A digital transmission technology that sends data over the existing cellular infrastructure, introduced in 1993.

Client A computer device, including PC, workstation, or terminal, that receives information from another computer device, typically a host system such as a larger server or mainframe.

Client/Server Computing A computing environment in which work is accomplished on more than one computer system, requiring the use of a network for communication. The workload and information is then distributed from the client to the server.

Database Management Systems (DBMS) The operating systems for database applications. A specialist piece of software that provides functionality for storing, updating, and retrieving information.

Distributed Computing Environment (DCE) One of the major accomplishments of the Open Software Foundation (OSF), DCE provides technology that serves as the basis of interoperability of distributed application development.

Fiber Distributed Data Interface (FDDI) A high-speed communications protocol used in local and wide area networking.

Integrated Services Digital Network (ISDN) A digital way of connecting to a wired telephone system.

International Standards Organization (ISO) A global organization, based in Geneva, Switzerland, that maintains a set of standards for quality assurance.

Internet Engineering Task Force (IETF) A voluntary organization that approves all worldwide standards for the Internet.

Internet Network Information Center (InterNIC) The organization that assigns domain names to each organization that connects to the Internet.

Internet Protocol (IP) This protocol supports host-to-host delivery of data packets across the network and is the layer that handles routing.

Legacy Term used to describe either systems or applications that are out-of-date in terms of current technology due to product or industry improvements.

Local Area Network (LAN) A method of connecting computer devices to communicate and work together within a limited geographic area, such as a workgroup or department within one building.

Modem Abbreviation for Modulator-Demodulator, an item of computing equipment used to encode and decode a digital data signal as a series of audio frequency tones suitable for transmission across communication lines.

Network Operating System (NOS) Software used to manage the communications between computers on LANs or WANs.

Object Linking and Embedding (OLE) A key technology for Microsoft, OLE is the technology direction for using applications that are composed of object components that combine at run time to provide a total solution.

Object Management Group (OMG) An industry consortium dedicated to developing standards and promoting object computing.

Object-Oriented (OO) A concept used to describe technologies that permit software components to be reused and/or combined in a modular fashion. Objects require a combination of data and code, inheritance and polymorphism.

Open Database Connectivity (ODBC) Microsoft's database access standard, which has become an industry standard. It permits client applications to interact with data and databases from multiple vendors.

Personal Communications Services (PCS) A generic term used to describe a set of wireless communication services.

Protocol A set of software standards used to regulate movement of data across the network.

Relational Database Management Systems (RDBMS) Database management that provides the use of logical references, such as department IDs and other data points, to provide flexibility in how data can be accessed.

Server A computer system, usually a larger system such as a mainframe or other host system, that provides services to other (client) computer systems. A server is usually not directly accessible for an end-user, who must use a client to access the server.

Server Side Includes (SSI) A way to dynamically update HTML documents with commands embedded in HTML documents that make Web pages do something different each time they are loaded. Unlike CGI scripts, SSIs are part of the server program and have no official standards. Some programs include support for text-only SSIs, while others also support SSI scripts.

Switched Multimegabit Data Service (SMDS) A connectionless packet-switching service, where each packet of information is addressed and sent independently to its destination.

Transmission Control Protocol/Internet Protocol (TCP/IP) A group of standard communication protocols used frequently in computer network communications. These were originally developed for use on the Internet.

Trusted client A client, or PC, used by a person who is authorized with the correct passwords so he or she can access sensitive corporate data.

X.25 An international recommendation defining a standard for the software interface and protocols to be used between a data communications network (over which data is carried as packets) and a data terminal equipment.

X.400 A international recommendation that describes a comprehensive architecture for store-and-forward communications.

Computer Technology Research Corp.

6 North Atlantic Wharf, Charleston, South Carolina 29401 U.S.A. • Tel: 803/853-6460; Fax: 803/853-7210

REPORT EVALUATION

Dear valued customer:

It is our continued desire and top priority to provide you with the most current and accurate computer technology information in our reports. Please assist us by taking a few minutes to answer the enclosed questionnaire. Your participation will help us to continue to provide professional service and quality reports to you. Please return the completed questionnaire by fax or mail. Feel free to attach additional sheets if you would like to add more comments. Your time and input are greatly appreciated.

Sincerely,

Edward R. Wagner

Edward R. Wagner
President

Report Title: _____

Customer Name: _____

Address/Phone: _____

_____

Rating System: 1=poor, 2=fair, 3=good, 4=above average, 5=outstanding	1	2	3	4	5
1. How would you rate your overall satisfaction with this report?	☐	☐	☐	☐	☐
2. How would you rate the informational content?	☐	☐	☐	☐	☐
3. How would you rate the technical content?	☐	☐	☐	☐	☐
4. Overall, how up-to-date is the report?	☐	☐	☐	☐	☐
How would you rate the quality of data provided regarding: a) product releases?	☐	☐	☐	☐	☐
b) price/performance data?	☐	☐	☐	☐	☐
c) product evaluations?	☐	☐	☐	☐	☐
d) management issues?	☐	☐	☐	☐	☐
5. How would you rate the quantity of illustrations?	☐	☐	☐	☐	☐
6. How would you rate the quality of illustrations?	☐	☐	☐	☐	☐
7. To what degree did this report provide the information which you were desiring to obtain on the subject matter?	☐	☐	☐	☐	☐

Continued on next page

Rating System: **1**=poor, **2**=fair, **3**=good, **4**=above average, **5**=outstanding.	**1**	**2**	**3**	**4**	**5**
8. How would you rate the readability of the report in terms of general appearance (type style, layout, etc.)?	☐	☐	☐	☐	☐
9. How would you rate the report's international coverage?	☐	☐	☐	☐	☐
10. To what extent will the material in this report figure into your decision-making?	☐	☐	☐	☐	☐
11. To what extent did you save time or money by reading this report? (Please explain briefly if possible)	☐	☐	☐	☐	☐

12. Is this the first CTR report you have purchased?	Yes ☐	No ☐
13. Would you purchase other CTR reports?	Yes ☐	No ☐
14. Would you recommend that other information technology professionals purchase this report?	Yes ☐	No ☐
15. Do you believe the information provided warrants the report's cost?	Yes ☐	No ☐
16. Were you satisfied with the service you received from our staff in fulfillment of your order?	Yes ☐	No ☐
17. Did your shipment arrive in good condition?	Yes ☐	No ☐
18. Were you satisfied with the delivery time of your shipment?	Yes ☐	No ☐

19. What additional information or topics would you have desired to see in this report that were not adequately covered?

20. What topics would you like to see us cover in future reports?

21. If you know of another individual whom you believe would be interested in receiving information concerning our report series, please list his/her full mailing address below:

Fax your completed questionnaire to: **(803) 853-7210**
or mail your completed questionnaire to: **Computer Technology Research Corp.**
6 North Atlantic Wharf
Charleston, SC 29401-2115 U.S.A.

Thank you for your time and input!